Credit Secrets

A Comprehensive Guide To Learn The Basics And Rules of Credit Cards, Hidden Secrets For Consumers And Benefits To Have Credit Cards To Make Life Easier

LEOPOLD BURKE

© **Copyright 2021 by LEOPOLD BURKE - All rights reserved.**

This document is geared towards providing exact and reliable information in regards to the topic and issue covered. The publication is sold with the idea that the publisher is not required to render accounting, officially permitted, or otherwise, qualified services. If advice is necessary, legal or professional, a practiced individual in the profession should be ordered.

- From a Declaration of Principles, which was accepted and approved equally by a Committee of the American Bar Association and a Committee of Publishers and Associations.

In no way is it legal to reproduce, duplicate, or transmit any part of this document in either electronic means or printed format. Recording of this publication is strictly prohibited, and any storage of this document is not allowed unless with written permission from the publisher. All rights reserved.

The information provided herein is stated to be truthful and consistent, in that any liability, in terms of inattention or otherwise, by any usage or abuse of any policies, processes, or directions contained within is the solitary and utter responsibility of the recipient reader. Under no circumstances will any legal responsibility or blame be held against the publisher for reparation, damages, or monetary loss due to the information herein, either directly or indirectly.

Respective authors own all copyrights not held by the publisher.

The information herein is offered for informational purposes solely and is universal as such. The presentation of the information is without a contract or any type of guarantee assurance.

The trademarks used are without any consent, and the publication of the trademark is without permission or backing by the trademark owner. All trademarks and brands within this book are for clarifying purposes only and are owned by the owners themselves, not affiliated with this document.

Contents

INTRODUCTION 9

CHAPTER 1: Learn About the Basics of Credit 13
- Credit vs. Debt 14
- The 5 C's of creditworthiness 16
- The four types of credit 17
- How to get credit 18
- Effective management of credit is critical 19
- Factors to look for when you apply for new credit 20
- Credit and its relation with credit reports 20
- Avoiding credit problems and credit abuse 20

CHAPTER 2: Federal Reserve Rules for Credit Cards 23
- Imposition of additional disclosure requirements 23
- Ways to choose the right credit card 28
- Checklist of what to look out for when choosing a credit card 30
- Finding cards with guaranteed approval 32

CHAPTER 3: Consumer Protection and Credit Legislation 35
- Federal laws regulating credit cards 36
- What debt collectors cannot do under the FDCPA 41
- What can collection agencies do? 44

CHAPTER 4: Origin and Advantages of Credit 46
- Origin of Credit 47
- First general-purpose charge card 48
- The Evolution of Credit Card Technology 49
- Who invented credit cards? 50
- Why was the credit card invented? 51
- How did credit cards become popular? 52

How have credit cards changed over the years?...52

Credit Card vs. Charge Card 63

Important Credit Card terms 64

CHAPTER 5: Secrets The Card Issuers Don't Want The Customers To Know 68

Your interest rate can change at any time 68

A late payment on one card could affect your APR on other cards..69

Balance transfers and cash advances are more expensive than you think 70

You have more power than you think 70

Annual fees are negotiable 71

There is no need to cancel the card..71

There is no need to spend money 72

The Vanilla Card Churn Strategy 72

The Paypal Load Strategy...72

By using your credit card, you can travel for free............................73

You can use the same card twice 73

You can get a signup bonus and close the account.........................73

You can get a lower interest rate if you ask.....................................73

Issuers make a ton of money from interchange..............................74

You can convert a card to one with no annual fee..........................74

A Perfect Credit Score is a Gateway to Free Travel 75

They're desperate for your business...75

They are willing to forgive you at least once....................................76

You can negotiate a lot more 77

They can only raise the rate for six months.....................................77

Interest backdating 78

Two-cycle billing 78

The right to setoff 78

Interest rate hikes are retroactive 78
Shortened due dates... 79
Eliminating grace periods 79
Disappearing benefits... 79
Fewer rights on debit cards 79
Double fees on cash advances 80
Misleading monthly minimums 80
Interest from day one 80

CHAPTER 6: Materialize Your Life Dreams By Building Excellent Credit Scores . 82

How Credit Works.. 83
Why Do You Need Good Credit?.. 85
Credit Scores 85
A Good VantageScore... 87
VantageScore 3.0 vs. other scoring models... 89
Learn to correctly use Credit Scores offered by three Credit Bureaus 90
Important facts you must know about the three main credit bureaus 93
What data do the credit bureaus include in your credit reports?..................... 94
How are your credit reports used? 95
How do credit bureaus get your information? 95
Why Are Credit Scores so Pivotal?... 96
Secrets of Credit Scores 97
FICO® Score Factors.. 98
Information not considered by Credit Scores.. 99

CHAPTER 7: Creative Ways to Make Money while Using the Credit Card 100

Earn credit card bonuses... 104
Use your card every day 105
Use a balance transfer credit card to pay down debt 105
Use a 0% APR card.. 105

Savings	106
The organization is the first step towards getting rich	106
Leverage credit to generate wealth	106
Become homeowner	106
Start a business	107
Venture capital	107
Look favorable when you are applying for a job	107
Get approval for handsome loans and healthy credit limits	107
Insurance	108
College	108
Utility Services	108
Skip the car rental insurance	109
Use the discount mall	109
Earn free travel or hotel stays	109
Shop on retail cardholder discount days	109
Extended Warranty Benefits	110
Take Advantage of Price Adjustments	110
Pay No Foreign Transaction Fees	110
Bottom line	111
Conclusion	**112**

INTRODUCTION

Credit means people's faith in your financial ability that facilitates them to give you different things such as goods, services, or money, hoping you would repay later on. For example, David has a watch worth $60, and Adam needs that watch but does not have the money to pay for it. Since Adam cannot pay straight away, David allows Adam to take the watch on $50 credit. Now Adam owns the credit watch. Furthermore, he has a $50 debt to David. Let us consider another example. Banks usually allow people to borrow money through a "credit card" or a "line of credit" with the hope that the person would return the amount in full or in installments. The bank normally charges interest on these transactions. If there is money in the bank in your account, it is your credit. In this case, you have faith that the bank will pay or return it to you whenever required. The bank would also pay to interest you for keeping money in your account. Similarly, if you receive an amount from somebody, then it is also considered credit. In broad terms, credit is referred to your ability to borrow. It's based on your mortgage servicing experience, so it points exactly how frequently you may borrow cash to buy products and services. There are several situations where you may make or break essential transactions with your credit. If you want to manage your credit intelligently, you must understand what credit is, what credit reports include, and how scores are generated. You also have to understand the importance of credit and different methods for boosting your credit score for a happy living. Credit represents your credibility for loan repayment based on your borrowing and repayment record. If you have a clear loan background or credit history, you get entitled to good credit. Strong credit shows to lenders that you are "creditworthy" or that you will be able to repay the borrowed money. It instills confidence in lending institutions that they will get back from you the loan principal plus some interest, which allows you more likely to get accepted for new credit (for example, a loan) with favorable terms, including low-interest rates or higher caps. Conversely, if your financial background shows that you can't repay your debts to lenders, you're considered to have bad credit. When you apply for a loan, having bad credit will harm you, as lenders may have less faith that you will repay it. If a lender needs to read a credit record to see your credit ranking, they seek that from what is regarded as a credit bureau (also classified as a credit-reporting agency). Credit bureaus gather all the data on your credit report from banks, card issuers, and other creditors, who submit your payment records voluntarily. Though credit bureaus store financial records on millions of customers, they might not hold as many records as you believe they do. Your taxable salary, for example, is not a feature of the standard credit report. Reporting companies either share or offer the details as you apply for a loan, or, for example, when a request is submitted from an employer who requires your consent before a report can be released. There are several credit bureaus, but the three bureaus have the biggest effect on the score, including TransUnion, Equifax, and Experian. The information must be correct in every credit bureau. When there are mistakes on the credit reports, you should call the specific bureau that produced the reports to rectify those mistakes to ensure that your credit application does not get rejected for no reason. The main record behind your rating is the credit history, and each credit bureau releases it. In up to seven years, credit records sum up different facets of your financial background. Credit reports are relevant as they act as the raw credit score data used by lenders to ascertain your creditworthiness and determine whether to extend a loan to you or not. Apart from your ratings, in making loan choices, lenders consider specific things in your credit reports. Before applying for a loan, you can and should check your credit reports to detect problems. You will receive one free full copy of your credit reports once a year under federal legislation. Lenders often use what are regarded as credit scores as the first move in determining whether to give you credit or not. They are three-digit scores created by a computer system that reads through your credit reports and searches for trends, attributes, and red flags in your background, which reduces it down to a numerical format that is simple to understand. Specific assessment methods independently measure credit ratings and evaluate results on various scales. Similarly, lenders will view and make lending decisions based on the credit score, irrespective of the scoring pattern. A higher score normally transforms you into a more creditworthy borrower, while a lower score represents a borrower with a poor background in borrowing. Although federal law gives you free credit reports, free credit scores are not guaranteed. However, credit scores can be purchased from credit bureaus, and some card issuers provide access to credit scoring services that allow you to view your credit score free of charge. This book discusses in detail credit, different types of credit, ways to build good credit scores, factors that are critical for building good credit, different credit bureaus that have an impact on your credit scores, information that credit bureaus want to keep secret, smart methods to get rid of long-standing debts, techniques to stretch credit scores by a good margin in a short period, ways to contest negative inquiries and false entries and more importantly credit secrets.

CHAPTER 1: Learn About the Basics of Credit

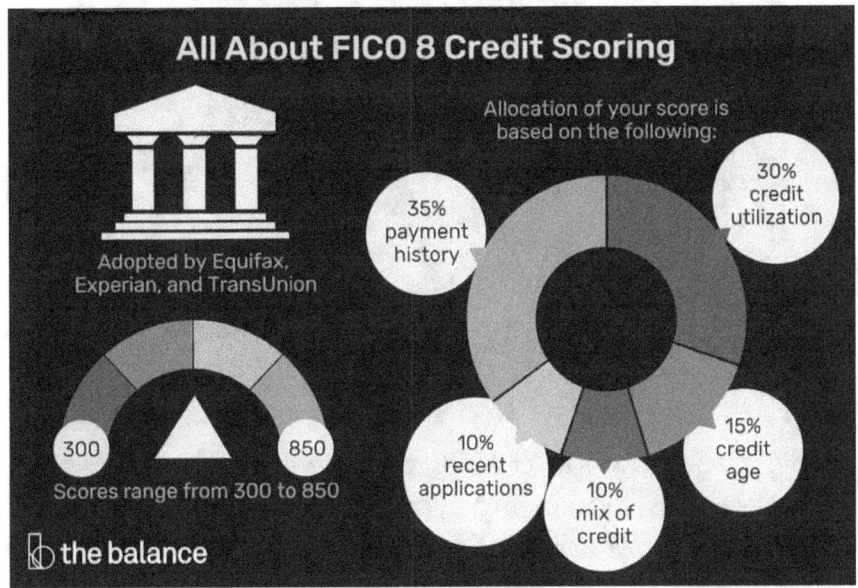

Credit is the process of borrowing money either from a bank or another financial institution to obtain goods. People used to go to the grocery store or other stores to purchase few things years ago. The customers would pay the business that has been keeping a record of their products, usually at the weekend or the end of the month. This was the credit at its most fundamental level. Credit cards, as well as loans, are the most common forms of credit today.

You walk into a store and pay for your purchases with your credit card. When you use a credit card, the bank pays for the products or services up front, and you pay the banks back at month's end. The process is the same whether you're buying a house or a car. The finance company or bank arranges money for a house or car. You then make a monthly payment to the bank or finance company until it's paid off, usually with interest.

Credit vs. Debt

It's critical to know the difference between debt and credit. Usually, credit is money that you take from a business. Debt refers to your current obligation to the particular establishment, which includes the amount borrowed (principal), as well as any interest & other fees. Credit is the amount of money you borrow from a lender and creditor, to put it another way. They lend you money with the expectation that you could repay them. When you take credit, you create a debit. It consists of the amount you borrowed as well as fees and interest. It's a debt that you owe.

The type of credit is dependent on the debt type

There are numerous different types of credit available. Furthermore, it usually depends on what one desires to use the credit for. The type of debt related to that type of credit is the most crucial consideration. Some forms of credit may appear to be distinct, but they are all identical. When it comes to credit in general, there are two types of debt to consider. These are secured & unsecured debts.

Secured debt

When you get credit in return for something, it's called a secured debt. You should

either provide collateral to the bank or have something that the bank may take from you if you don't pay back your loan on time. Given below are few examples of the secured debt:

- Secured credit cards
- Car loans
- Home loans

When you apply for a secured credit card, you deposit with the bank, which serves as collateral. If you don't pay your bills, the creditor will take your deposit to pay off the debt. Home loans are a type of secured credit. If you don't pay the mortgage, a bank can take your house & resell it in most states. Consider the housing crisis that took place at the beginning of the Great Recession. During the period above, all of the houses were in foreclosure or were being sold by banks. Car loans are a type of secure credit since cars are tangible assets with a monetary value. Your car may be repossessed &/or given to the bank if you do not pay your car loan. Understand that failing to pay or defaulting in any of these situations will significantly impact the credit reports.

Unsecured debt

Unsecured debts are the credit granted to you based on your credit worthiness. The financial institution essentially lends you money in the hope that you shall repay it, sometimes with some interest.

The 5 C's of creditworthiness

Banks look at the "Five C's of creditworthiness" to succeed for the most types of secure credit as well as all of the unsecured creditors. The majority of the 5 C's are concerned with your past ways of handling and managing money & loans. This gives lenders a better idea of how likely it is that they will be repaid. The five Cs are woven with the criteria of each bank. Depending on their lending model, lenders & creditors put diverse values on numerous areas; these C's provide you few things to ponder before deciding to take out the new credit line with the bank.

Credit History/Character

To form an opinion regarding your personality, a lender will consider several factors, including your credit history. Whereas a credit union or a more minor or a local bank may be more concerned with your character, taking references and reputation into account before deciding on a loan, a big bank will typically look at the credit history as well as your abilities to repay loans on time.

Capacity

Capacity is at times viewed as the "cash flow." Capacity is, in reality, the ability to pay back the loans based on your annual income. It also looks at your debt-to-income ratio & more. It demonstrates to the bank that you have the financial strength to repay the loan.

Capital

Capital is usually an aspect of businesses. However, capital shows the bank what amount of money investors or you have committed in the business.

Collateral

A bank, similar to the secured loan, will glance at what assets are tangible and used as collateral if you default on a loan.

Conditions

All These are external factors that may affect your abilities to repay the loan. Your job market and business may influence the type & amount of the loan that you receive.

The four types of credit

There are various credit terms for secured & unsecured debts which explain the particular kind of credits you're getting & how you'll have to repay them. It includes the amount you must pay every month & whether it varies. Give below are different type of credits:

Revolving credit

The type of credit is similar to that of a credit card or a home equity line of credit (H.E.L.O.C). You have the set borrowing limit & can borrow up to the amount at any time, often while compensating it back or making monthly payments to pay anything you owe.

Installment credit or fixed loans

Car loans, along with mortgages, as well as house payments, are instances of installment loans. You borrowed a certain amount of capital you had to repay after some time (usually years). The total amount owed was divided into monthly payments and interest, & you now pay a set amount for each month till the loan is paid in full. The installment loan does not allow you to borrow more capital.

Open credit and closed credit

An open credit line is a credit line that you can use to borrow money when you need it. A closed credit account is one in which you are given a fixed amount of money up front. A home-based equity loan, for example, is a closed line of credit as you receive a fixed amount of capital after you've been approved. A HELOC, on the other hand, is the open credit line. You could even borrow a specific amount, but you are not required to use the entire amount. Revolving payments are expected with open credit, whereas installment payments are every day with closed credit.

How to get credit

We shall now tell you the ways of getting credit. For many individuals, obtaining credit begins at an early age. Several parents place their kids on credit cards to help them establish a good credit history. Individuals can do this if the account's primary holder of account includes them as some authorized user.

It tends to help have a bank account if and only if you need to get credit independently. Although it is not a vital component of the credit history, that can help with 1 of the five Cs of credit worthiness: character. You are also demonstrating capacity if you may account in bank & automatic deposits with the recurring income. One other option's to apply for a secure credit card that reports to all three credit bureaus. You'll need to deposit at first, but it'll help you develop a +ve credit account over time (if you pay it off every month & keep your spendings low) and open the door to more credit. Cell phones, as well as store credit cards, are two other options for obtaining credit. Both require much fewer credits to be accepted or some down payment when your credit may especially be bad. Down payment, once again, is meant to secure a loan if you may default.

Meanwhile, each of the credit lines you start or create should help you build a positive credit history. A third viable option is to get a co-signing person on loan. It can be risky for a co-signer, but it can be advantageous if you repay the loan. You and the co-signers are jointly responsible for the entire loan amount, and you don't want to harm the co-signer's credit or finances by defaulting on your loans.

Effective management of credit is critical

Whatever options you choose, it's critical to stay on top of your monthly payment and keep your credit card balance at or around 0. This will have a positive effect on your credit score. Set up involuntary payments with your accounts, so you don't have to worry about missing a payment.

Factors to look for when you apply for new credit

Just Make sure to read the terms as well as the conditions once applying for new credit. What are the chances of getting approved depending on your credit score? What are the current rates of interest? What are the terms of repayment? Shall you be penalized if you attempt to pay the loan off sooner than expected or compensate more than the minimum payment? Before signing on loan or opening new credit, ensure to read the fine print that can be extensive.

Credit and its relation with credit reports

Accounts accumulate on the credit report as you develop your credit. Experian, TransUnion, and Equifax are the three reporting credit agencies that keep track of your credit. Each bureau keeps track of your credit applications, approvals, and payment history. Every credit bureau has its algorithm for determining your creditworthiness to other moneylenders. Your report of credit will also reveal how long you've had credit. All of the indicators above aid lenders in achieving their five Cs. If you desire to remain creditworthy and gain access to new credit, it's critical to keep your credit and credit reports in good standing.

Avoiding credit problems and credit abuse

The most crucial aspect of having credit is sustaining it. You are required to pay off an installment loan at least a predefined amount every month with an installment loan. While paying down the loan will keep the account in good standing. Revolving credit or credit cards is where many people get themselves into trouble. When you have a higher borrowing limit, you may find yourself spending more money than you can afford to pay back each month or in a reasonable period. Your spending could even quickly spiral out of control, resulting in monthly interest payments, which are far higher than you can afford. If you can't control your spending and learn to budget, you'll end up with credit card debt and eventually lousy credit. If you do end up with credit card debt, there are options available to help you repair your credit. Credit repair and debt management services can help you gain control of your debt and develop a plan to repay the loans and rebuild the credit.

CHAPTER 2: Federal Reserve Rules for Credit Cards

On 22nd February 2010, the Federal Reserve Board of Governors issued new regulations requiring credit card companies to safeguard consumers. The new regulations require the disclosure of fees, rates, and limits to consumers and notice changes in fees and services. It's worth noting that credit cards & banks are not subject to usury laws.

Imposition of additional disclosure requirements

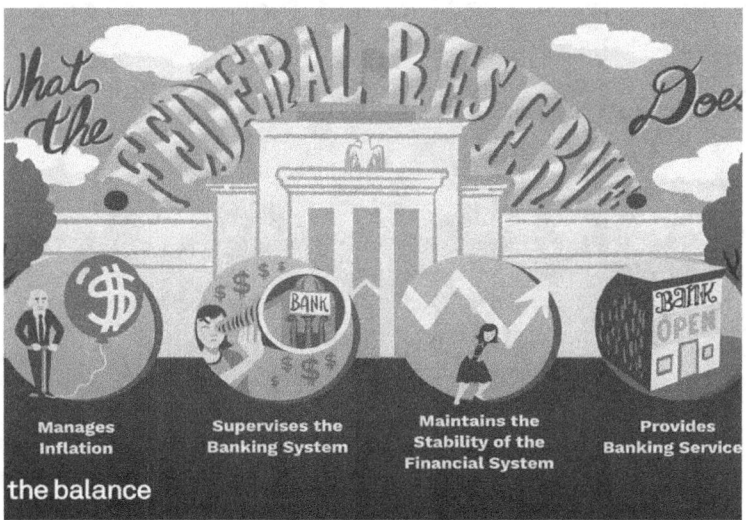

Following are the additional requirements that Federal Reserve has imposed.

Forty-five days are written notice

It is mandatory for credit cards company to give the customer 45 days prior notice (written) before they:

- Enhance their interest rate

- Make changes in certain fees (like advance cash fees, annual fees, or late fees) that apply to the account
- Introduce other important changes to the card terms

If the credit card companies want to change the terms of the card, you must be given options to cancel before the certain fees increases go into effect. If you choose that option, credit card companies may close the account and, subject to certain restrictions, increase the monthly payments to pay any outstanding amount. For example, they can make you pay off your balance in 5 years or double the percentage of the balance utilized to calculate the minimum payment that will lead to much faster repayment compared to under terms of the account. If there are variable interest rates linked to an index, the company is not required to give you 45 days' notice if:

- index rises, the company is not required to give you notice before the rate rises.
- The introductory rates expire and go back to the previously revealed "go-to" rate
- Your rate rises as a result of the workout agreement in which you struggled to make the payment on time.

Information on the minimum period for paying off the balance

The credit card's monthly bill should include how long it will take to pay off the balance when making the minimum payments. This must advise how much you'd need to pay each month to pay off the balance in 3 years. E.g., let's suppose you owe 3,000$ and the interest rate's 14.4 percent, the bill will most likely look like this-

        Newest balance   3,000.00$

        least payment due   90.00$

        Payment's due date   20/4/12

Late Payment Warning

If you don't receive the minimum payments by the date mentioned above, you might have to pay a late fee of $35, plus your APRs might be enhanced up to Penalty APRs of 28.99 percent.

Minimum Payment Warning

Whether you decide to make minimum payment only for each period, you'll pay extra in interest. Moreover, you will take more time to pay off the balance.

New rules on rates, fees, and limits

For first-year, there will be no interest rate increases. For the first twelve months after opening an account, your credit card company cannot raise your rate. However, there are a few exceptions:

- If the credit card has an interest rate that is variable and is linked to an index, your rate may increase as the index rises.
- If there's a situation of the introductory rate, it must remain in effect for a minimum of six months; otherwise, your rate

may switch back to "go-to" rates disclosed when the card is received.

- If you pay your bill late for more than sixty days, the rate may increase.
- If you do not make the payments as the agreement in a workout agreement, your rate may increase.

Increased rates can be applied only to new charges

If the credit card company decides to raise the interest rate in the first year and, the latest rate will only apply to the new charges. If you have a balance, then your previous interest rates will be applied to it.

Restrictions applicable on over-the-limit transactions

It would help if you informed the credit card companies that you want transactions that will exceed the credit limit to be permitted. Or else, if the transaction may push you over your limit, it might be declined. You cannot be charged an over-the-limit fee if you don't choose for over-limit transactions, but instead, the credit card company permits 1 to go by. - The credit card company can only charge you one fee per billing cycle if you choose to allow transactions that exceed the credit limit. You have the power to rescind the opt-in any time you want to.

Caps on high-fee cards

Now, If the credit card company charges fees (like annual fees or an application fee), the total of those fees can't exceed 25% of your initial credit limits. E.g., if your initial credit limit's US$500, your first-year fees cannot exceed $125. This restriction does not apply to penalty fees, like late payment penalties.

Protections for underage consumers

So If you're under the age of 21, you'll have to show you can make the payments or a cosigner to open credit card

accounts. If you're under the age of 21 and have a card with a cosigner, your cosigner must agree to an enhancement in credit limit in writing.

Standard payment dates and times

The credit card company must deliver or mail the credit card bills at least twenty-one days before the due date.

- Furthermore, the due date must be the same every month. For instance, your payment should always be due on the 10th or should be due on the month's last day.
- On the due date, the cut-off payment time could not be earlier than five pm.
- If the payment is due on a holiday or weekend (when the company is closed), you'll have until the next business day to make the payment. For instance, if the payment is due on Sunday,15th, it will be received before five p.m. on Monday, the 16th.

Payments should be directed to the highest interest balances

If you pay more than the minimum amount due on the credit card bill, the excess must be applied to the outstanding amount with the most significant interest rate. There's one exception to this rule. If you bought something on a credit card with deferred interest plans, e.g., no interests if paid fully by April 2012, the credit card company must let you apply extra funds to the deferred interests balance first. Otherwise, the credit card company should apply the total payment to the deferred interest rates balance first for two billing cycles before the end of the deferred interest period.

No two-cycle (double-cycle) billing

The Creditcard companies could only charge interest on balances that have been carried over from the previous billing cycle.

Ways to choose the right credit card

A credit card is a card that lets you borrow money against a credit line, otherwise known as the credit limit for the card. You use the card to make basic transactions reflected on your bill; the bank pays the merchant, and later, you pay the bank when you receive your bill. You'll get interested charged on your purchases. Don't carry debt forward from month to month to prevent interest charges. Credit cards have high-interest rates and can affect your credit card score and payment history. Paying on time and in full will help you avoid interest and late fees and keep your credit score better and even more vital. You run the chance, with a credit card, of spending outside your income. For example, the credit card's maximum cap, a credit limit of $1,000, doesn't suggest you can handle any spending. Credit cards offer additional purchase insurance and may facilitate the request for a refund or return.

Nonetheless, specific incentives are being diluted or eliminated by several businesses. To understand the benefits, you should carefully read your credit card's disclosure information. Credit cards will help protect you in an emergency, allowing you a month to return the cash until the bill is due. This safety net may

help you catch yourself trying to budget for anything significant before a refund comes in, so be careful: based on the immediate spending credit, you are setting up for high interest because you cannot cover it in full by the due date. A safer option will be to keep an emergency fund on hand. If you want to take advantage of credit card loyalty schemes, obtaining a credit card is the safest choice. Yet this method just operates in your favor if every month you pay out the balance in full. You can save in rewards if you find yourself carrying a balance, but you end up paying as much or more in interest. When you are trying to build up your credit score, use your credit card carefully. Paying the payment on time would build a record of sound, creditworthy conduct recorded to the credit bureaus and displayed in the credit score. Identity theft and misuse when using payment cards are threats to protect against. That's why you must know what safeguards your card provides. You run the risk of compromising your card information upon its loss or theft. In such an event, you need to contact the relevant bank quickly.

Many institutions have a number you can dial around the clock. The sooner you dial, the more potent. Upon claiming that something is lost or robbed, you won't be responsible for false transactions made with the ATM. Follow up with a formal reply via letter or email once you have reported for the lost card. Scan your statement very closely for payments you did not make and disclose them to the bank. Track the credit report to ensure it has not compromised your identity. When your payment card has been stolen, you can opt to block your account to further secure it against more theft. Lots of credit cards are available, so look around and find the one that better suits you. You need to think about the purpose you need the credit card for. It may be ordering items online or on holiday, paying your bills, spreading the expense of a transaction, or borrowing money.

Checklist of what to look out for when choosing a credit card

Mentioned below is a checklist of some things to contemplate upon while choosing a credit card:

Annual Percentage Rate (APR)

This is the expense of paying on loan, especially if you do not pay off the whole balance every month. For various cards, you will check the APR, which will help you pick the cheapest. You should also evaluate specific issues involving the cards, such as fees, costs, and rewards.

Minimum repayment

When you don't pay off your balance every month, you'll be forced to add back a sum. Usually, that is ascribed to 3 percent of the balance.

Annual fee

Each year some cards charge a fee for using the card. The fee is applied to the sum owed, so you may continue to incur interest on both the transaction and the spending until you pay it in full.

Charges

Find out what other costs are related to the account in the credit agreement. Generally, you'll be charged for exceeding the credit limit, using the card overseas, and late payments.

Introductory interest rates

This is where you start paying a low-interest rate or absolutely none. After a certain period, the rate increases instead. It might, for example, rise after six months or from a specific date. You will often see a rate of introduction for balance transfers. If you compare cards, look at how long the introductory rate will last and the rate of interest to which it changes at the end of the introductory period.

Loyalty points or rewards

Based on the sum you spent, the points add up, and you can then use them to purchase products. This is especially true for retail shops. Evaluate when and where to use the rewards, and decide how likely you are to use them.

Cash back

Depending on how much you spend, you get a chance of a money refund on your account. Check the probability of your qualification for the cash back. This may only apply, for example, if you pay your balance in full every month. A lower interest rate could well be a better deal.

Comparing cards

When you are provided credit card details, it will have a summary box with standard critical card information. This should include a period for which no interest would be

charged, interest rate, and other charges. This helps you to evaluate various cards quickly.

Finding cards with guaranteed approval

If you see a card marketed as guaranteed, that does not mean it is available to everyone. It may, however, be a little easier to get a standard credit card.

Each card issuer has essential criteria for welcoming a new client. "Guaranteed approval," when it comes to credit cards, means you'll be approved as long as you meet certain conditions. Those conditions are typically minimal, fortunately. For example, you can need to provide your name and contact details, have a checking account and confirm a defined income amount.

Guaranteed approval vs. Easy approval

Most card companies will not offer the guaranteed approval. Instead, they use terminology, which means that you will easily be welcomed. Typically, you will see phrases such as "no minimum credit score" or "see if you prequalify." You may still be denied the card, but you may have good prospects than most other providers. Generally speaking, credit cards that offer "guaranteed approval" are designed for those with fair to poor credit. This ensures that they would hold the same characteristics you might like to see in terrible credit cards. A few examples are high annual fees, high purchase APRs, lack of rewards, and punishment in the form of penalty fees. These cards cannot stack up to a regular personal card if you place them next to each other.

If you are considering these cards, you should be trying to restore your reputation. If that is the case, it is recommended to have a secured card than a guaranteed approval card.

Unsecured cards with guaranteed approval

The eligibility criterion for unsecured cards is fairly simple:

- You need to be a US resident
- You should be at least 18 years old.
- You must concur with the card provider's terms and conditions.
- You need to have a valid payment method, namely a debit card, credit card, or checking account.
- You have to give evidence that you will make a specified monthly payment, mainly if you use your card's total credit line.
- You should be able to pay the enrollment fees.

Secured cards with guaranteed approval

Most secured card providers do not offer genuinely guaranteed approval like unsecured card providers. Few providers guarantee approval as long as they can verify your residence, identity, and payment capability. You also need to have a valid checking account.

CHAPTER 3: Consumer Protection and Credit Legislation

Various laws protect cardholders in various ways, including preventing discrimination in lending, allowing you to correct errors on credit reports, requiring issuers to give notice before significant changes in terms, and more. It's critical to understand your rights as a consumer cruising the credit world. Many federal laws give you certain rights when it comes to your financial and credit activity.

Federal laws regulating credit cards

Also, there are federal regulations that protect your interests when dealing with credit card companies. The following are some of the most significant laws as well as protections to be aware of:

The Truth in Lending Act

It allows customers to make credit card decisions. Details about the cost (terms) of credit must be reported under federal law. On the documents they submit, creditors are expected to list all of the contractual costs and average percentage rates. Deliberate violators will face administrative penalties as well as civil penalties, according to the legislation. It also helps protect customers' credit cards from being used fraudulently. When a card is lost or stolen, the maximum amount a customer pays $50.

The Fair Credit and Charge Card Disclosure Act

It necessitates a box's inclusion on credit card applications that defines the card's core features and costs.

The Credit Card Act of 2009

It developed new credit card rules and amended existing ones, such as regulations that prohibit unfair credit card practices. This law requires that additional information be included in the disclosure box, limits fees, and rate increases, and requires consistency in payment dates and times. Over-the-credit-limit charges are one issue addressed by the new rules. According to the law, customers must notify their credit card issuer if they want the company to agree to allow transactions that will exceed the credit limit on their accounts. The company may not charge an over-the-limit fee if the cardholder has advised the credit card issuer to acknowledge over-the-limit charges on his or her account. Any purchase that would allow an account to go over the credit limit would be denied unless the

cardholder has advised the credit card provider to allow over-the-limit charges.

The Equal Credit Opportunity Act (ECOA)

ECOA prohibits creditors from discrimination against you and declining to grant the credits based on:

- Race
- Sex
- Marital status
- National origin
- Religion
- Age

Creditors have the right to request this kind of information. However, they cannot use it to make decisions. Creditors must, for example, consider a dependable form of public assistance, like disability payment, in almost the similar way they might any other source of income. You get legal rights to be informed why credit has been denied to you. If you're denied credit, the lender would then send you a letter explaining how you were turned down.

The Fair Credit Reporting Act (FCRA)

When it comes to credit reports, Fair Credits Reporting Act (the FCRA) helps protect privacy rights and gives you the tools to correct some errors. Most importantly, FCRA gives the right to inspect the credit report & have any inaccurate information removed. FCRA also regulates who has access to the credit report & for what purpose. In general, somebody can only get the credit report if they have legitimate reasons to be doing so, or even if you ask one on their behalf. Creditors checking prospective borrowers' credit reports, employers handling the employee benefits issues, and insurers checking credit before issuing policy are legitimate business reasons. You may opt out of receiving pre-screened or pre-approved credits and insurance and unsolicited offers in the mail under the Fair Credit Reporting Act (FCRA). If your opinion changes after opting out, you may opt back in using the same procedure. You always have the right to get any credit report errors corrected. You may easily file a dispute with the relevant consumer's credit bureau via the internet. The agency must conduct an investigation and make the essential changes or corrections. The Credit report agencies must provide lists of who is receiving copy of report that contains incorrect information and the sources of any incorrect information. The agency should re-issue the corrected credit reports to any of the lenders who obtained the credit reports within the last six months and any employer who did receive your credit reports within the last two years once these errors have been corrected.

The Fair Debt Collection Practices Act (FDCPA)

You must pay your debts. Your creditors may hand over

outstanding debts to a debt collector if you don't. You have some rights still if this happens.

The Fair Credit Billing Act (FCBA)

According to the FCBA, card issuers must credit the payments promptly & correct any errors on the credit card bills without harming the credit score. You can also dispute billing errors & stop payments from purchasing goods damaged with a credit card.

Credit CARD Act (CARD Act)

A majority of consumer protection provisions were included in CARD Act, which was enacted in 2009. Such as, the law prohibits credit card issuers from raising the interest rate on the existing balances & demands them to give you forty-five days' notice before actually changing the terms of your card, like raising the interest rate on the new transactions. The Card companies should also deliver or mail the bill minimum of 21 days well before payment's due, with the same due date every month.

The Fair Credit and Charge Card Disclosure Act

The legislation requires the lenders to divulge the costs & features of credit you're applying for, such as annual percentage rates that will be charged on the account balances, minimum grace time for purchases, annual fees, most minor finance charges, cash advance transaction fees, and some penalties for the late payments or charging much more than the stated credits limit.

What to do when a credit card issuer sues you

Ignoring debt would be a bad thing you could do. However,

some customers fall behind. The Others are challenged with debts they had forgotten about. Others receive notices of debts they thought they had paid already or that they owe to someone else. So Whatever the case may be, if you start receiving notices about debt, you must act quickly.

Pursuing the Debt

Collection methods used by credit card issuers are varied. They go after debtors with own the in-house collection department and law firms of 3rd-party and collections agencies. You're legally bound to pay your debt regardless of how they pursue it, and if you don't, the creditor could even take legal actions against you.

When will a creditor sue a debtor?

Mainly, if the debt is less than 1,000$, you are unlikely to be sued. If you have a large debt, your chances of being sued are greater. You make yourself a perfect target for legal action if you disregard repeated collection attempts. Consumers often ignore collection letters as well as phone calls. They may be

disgusted or frightened. Or they may not believe it to be true. If you don't react and debt is significant enough, you can anticipate suing. Pocket service is permitted in some states. This means that if you don't respond to debt correspondence, the creditor can get default judgments against you, even if the creditor hasn't filed a lawsuit against you yet. Some consumers believe the letter attempts intimidation because it lacks official-looking documentations from a court of law. Unfortunately, in some states, a lawyer's letter carries as much weight as a complaint, and if the debtor ignores it, a default judgment could enter against him.

What can the debtor do?

Depending on the specifics of the situation, a consumer who is being investigated for the debt collection could even take various actions. Making a payment is not a good idea. It is especially crucial if you're confident the debt isn't yours. Many courts will consider making payments toward debt to be an affirmation that debt's valid. Request that the creditor confirms the debt. The creditor has thirty days to submit proof that the debt's valid as well as belongs with you after you request it. If the creditor is unable to do so, they will be unable to obtain judgments against you. The collectors of Debt are frequentlyincorrect. They frequently go after the zombie debt, which is debt that you've paid but isn't yours or has passed the collection statute of the limitations. It's sometimes enough to ask them to validate the debt to close the case. Speak with a consumer lawyer. If you Even don't have the funds to hire an attorney, seek advice from one. Many lawyers would take your complaint on a contingency basis, especially if there's a severe breach of the Fair Debt Collections Practices Act, as a victory in the court will cover legal fees. However, once a creditor is notified that the attorney supports you, the creditor is prohibited from contacting you again. So They should first communicate with you through your attorney. If debts are all yours, so settling those with the help of an attorney may be way less expensive than visiting the court and having a judgment entered against you. The fees charged by attorneys vary greatly. Rates for the debt settlement services are frequently linked to the amount of the debt to be settled. Attorneys are subject to the same regulations as the for-profit debts settlement companies, & they are not permitted to begin charging an upfront fee concerning debts settlement services.

What debt collectors cannot do under the FDCPA

The debt collectors have to comply with the following:

- When collecting these debts, debt collectors are prohibited from employing deceptive, unfair, or abusive practices.
- Debt collectors can only contact you between the hours of 8 a.m. and 9 p.m., and they should identify themselves while calling you.
- Debt collectors are not permitted to oppress, harass or abuse you, nor are they permitted to keep lying to you.
- Debt collectors are not allowed to meet you at work if your employer prohibits it.
- If you ask debt collectors to stop bothering you in writing, they must comply.

Can debt collection agencies harass you?

Do you ever feel as if the debt collectors are pursuing you? Even Though the debt collectors compensate for the persistence in trying to reclaim funds (& you've presumably not kept up the end of the bargain if you've been contacted by 1), the Fair Debt Collection Practices Act mandates that all the debt collectors follow specific rules of engagement (FDCPA). Given below are legal regulations concerning what the debt collectors cannot and can do.

They must maintain your privacy

Debt collectors may use a third party to validate the correct contact information under the FDCPA, but they can't mention you owe the money. However, if debt collectors are specifically asked, they must state the company's name because they work, but they cannot mention that they're contacting to collect a debt. As a result, any mailed correspondence, whether in a letter or on the envelope, cannot "declare" that you owe a debt. Debt collectors aren't permitted to send any postcards.

They must inform you about them

Once debt collectors have made direct contact with you, FDCPA requires them to send you written notice within 5 days, which details the amount owed & the name of the creditor owed unless you've already paid the debt in question. Also, the letter must contain few statements which fundamentally outline rights, such as. The fact that until you dispute the debt within thirty days of getting the letter, the creditor assumes it is valid. The letter must also state if you notify the debt collector in writing within 30 days of receiving the letter, they will provide the name as well as address of the original creditor provide it is different from the current creditor; they will not be able to contact you until they have presented the information because of your requests.

They cannot harass you

Debt collectors are prohibited from calling you repeatedly, using aggressive language or even profanity, "coercing" payment of a debt or contacting you at an "unusual place or time" that is known as being "inconvenient" under the FDCPA. Though the regulations are vague, they essentially mean they can't show up at your workplace, your child's school, or anywhere else. Similarly, they cannot contact me by phone before 8 am. or after 9 pm.; if the employer doesn't permit personal calls, they aren't permitted to contact at work at any time. If the debt collector is aware that you're working with an attorney to manage your finances, she or he is needed to directly contact an attorney. The debt collector is not allowed to contact you unless your attorney responds on behalf of you within "reasonable time." Though sending debtors away won't make the debt go away, the FDCPA allows a debtor's parents, spouse, children (especially if the debtor is minor), or even executor (if debtor's deceased) to notify debt collectors in writing to stop communicating with them. Once the collector receives the letter, they cannot contact the debtor except to inform them that further the collection efforts have been discontinued or that the collection agency wants to invoke a specified remedy that may include a lawsuit.

What can collection agencies do?

Although collections agencies may assist small-scale business owners and lenders in recovering funds that are owed to them, they are only paid when they're successful in collecting. As a result, they can be assertive and break the rules. So Here are facts and myths about your rights, as well as a debt collector.

They can reach out to you

Fair Debt Collections Practices Act (the FDCPA) has been enacted to regulate the debt collection process. When they could contact (only between 8 am. and 9 pm. local time) and where they can call are two rules. Collectors are not allowed to contact you at work if the employer does not allow private calls, e.g., If you've hired legal counsel to handle the debt (& debt collector is aware of this), the debt collector must contact the lawyer directly. Although refusing to take or respond to debt collectors' phone calls and letters will not make debt (or even them) go away, the FDCPA states that consumers also have legal right to refuse to take or respond to debt collectors' phone calls & letters. They should be open and honest when it comes to sharing information. The Debt collectors were required by law to recognize themselves as debt collectors & explain why they are contacting you. They've five days after speaking with you to provide the written information about the collection. This also includes the amount owed as well as the creditor.

They can be persistent

If you pay what you owe, debt collectors effectively compensated for the persistence. Expect to be contacted by a debt collector several times, but be aware that you have rights. Collectors are prohibited from using aggressive language, even profanity, or other harassing behavior, including repeatedly calling, under the FDCPA. If you believe they've gone too far, you have the legal rights to send cease & desist letters to the collection agency, stating you don't want to be contacted for the debt any longer. Therefore, the debt collector should stop contacting about the debt owed once they obtain that communication (which you should send certified mail). You could even file a complaint with Consumer Financial Protections Bureau if they don't comply.

They cannot force you to do anything

The job of a debt collector's to collect the money you owe and ideally gather it in full. A debt collector, on the other hand, cannot force you to pay your debts or impose a deadline on whether or not you do so until the creditor sued you & won Writ of the Garnishment And if this happens, then the wages can be deducted and then used in repaying debts, based on debt type & state where you work). By the time a collector is involved, the deadline that mattered is the due date's irrelevant in terms of the credit score and credit report.

They can report the collection to the credit reporting agencies

Debt collectors can pull your credit reports as well as disclose the collection accounts to credit bureaus. Collectors can use the credit report to help them collect debts under the Fair Credit Reporting Act. That means they'll know the place you live & if you can repay with an unused credit card.

CHAPTER 4: Origin and Advantages of Credit

We all make use of credit. You use credit every time you use the phone, turn on a light, or turn on the air conditioning, just as you do when you use a credit card or take out a loan. Credit is a contract that allows you to receive goods, services, and money now and pay for them later. You are the only one who can decide how you will spend all your money and whether or not you will use credit. These choices should be made based on the ability to repay credit debt rather than what you want to buy right now. Lenders, retailers, and service suppliers, commonly known as creditors, award credit based on their belief that you can be entrusted to pay back what you borrowed, along with any potential lending costs. You are considered creditworthy or have "strong credit," to the degree that borrowers find you worthy of their trust.

Origin of Credit

Thousands of years have passed since merchants used credit to assist their customers in financing purchases. Seeds, for example, were sold to farmers with payment terms that allowed for payment after harvest. The Code of Hammurabi, which was named after Babylon's ruler from 1792 to 1750 B.C. in what is now Iraq, is one of the earliest written examples of a credit system. These laws established guidelines for borrowing and repaying money and the amount of interest that could be charged. A loan was traditionally a financial agreement between one borrower and one creditor or merchant. A customer could "run a tab" with an individual merchant in more modern times, and it is called a revolving line of credit. This type of credit could be continuously borrowed against and has no specified payoff date. This is the same as a store credit card linked to a more extensive payment system.

1792 BC - Modern day Iraq

Seeds were sold to farmers. The terms allowed farmers to pay after the harvest

1930's - Metal Cards

Medals and coins ultimately took the shape of rectangular metal cards

1940's - Air Travel Card

Air Travel card facilitated travelers in the 1940s and 1950s to buy tickets on credit from different airlines

1950's - First Modern Credit Card

Diner's Club rolled out its card in the 1950s. Diners cards are commonly recognized as the first modern credit card. It can easily be used at several retailers

1980's - Magnetic Strips

Several cards used to have a magnetic stripe on the back. This magnetic strip was easily read by specialized computer equipment, which was considered to be the most advanced system of the time

1990's - EMV Chips

EMV chip technology was developed. It remained in effect in the U.S. for several years.

2008 - Mobile Wallet

The Apple app store introduced mobile wallets.

The Merging of "Credit" and "Card"

Companies progressed on the idea of revolving credit in the late 19th and early 20th centuries by including a physical object which could be used to quickly access their customer accounts. Some came in the form of coins or medallions bearing the merchant's name and logo and the customer's account number. Like many credit card transactions in the twentieth century, the merchant would imprint the coin or medal on the customer's sales slip. These coins and medals were transformed into rectangular metal cards known as Charge-Plates in the 1930s, which looked like a cross between a credit card and a military dog tag.

First general-purpose charge card

Only just a few things were missing before anyone could create the modern payment card, with consumers carrying rectangular metal cards which they could use to make purchases. Someone had to first come up with a financial instrument that could be used to make multiple charges at different merchants. The Air Travel Card, which also allowed travelers in the 1940s and 1950s to buy tickets on credit from multiple airlines, was an early example. Diners Club founders Ralph Schneider and Frank McNamara invented the modern payment card in 1950. This was the first general-purpose charge card, but it needed consumers to pay the entire balance of their statement each month. Customers were later allowed to carry a balance on their cards, thanks to American Express and others. This was the final piece of innovation needed to create the financial product we now know as a credit card.

The Evolution of Credit Card Technology

Credit cards are a vital component of the American economy, for better or worse. According to Experian's State of the Credit report, the average American had 3.1 credit cards with an average balance of $6,354 and 2.5 retail credit cards with an extra balance of $1,841 at the end of 2017. But everyone wants to know that when the credit cards were invented? According to the Federal Reserve, the total credit card debt in the United States surpassed $1 trillion last year. But have you ever considered how we came to be in this position? Perhaps the most remarkable aspect of credit cards is how quickly they've become indispensable in modern capitalism. The modern credit card can be traced back to Diners Club's founding in 1950, which was the first charge card that could be used at multiple retailers. Diners Club was a modern take on an old tradition. Credit cards initially functioned similarly to previouscoins, medals, and plates. Merchants would imprint the card that would be familiar to anyone who recalls how everyday credit card purchases were in the 1990s. By the 1980s, however, many cards had a magnetic stripe on the back that could be read by advanced computer equipment, which was cutting-edge at the time.

A magnetic stripe is considered primitive by today's standards. This is because the information stored on it isn't even encrypted. Credit cards with embedded computer chips are displacing magnetic stripes in the same way that imprinting displaced magnetic stripe readers. EMV smart chips are embedded computer chips that enable encrypted two-way verification between a merchant's credit card terminal and the payment processing network. This technology was developed in the 1990s and has been widely adopted in Europe for 20 years. However, America's migration to EMV-enabled cards and readers has only taken place in the last five years. Compared to simple magnetic stripes, the encrypted communications make it much less vulnerable to hackers, and the computer chips are even more challenging for criminals to counterfeit. However, as wireless payment technologies are swiftly integrated into smartphones, watches, and other wearable platforms, some industry experts believe EMV smart chips' era may be short. Finally, many people envision a day when biometric authentication will allow customers to charge purchases with their fingerprints or retinal scans rather than carry around a card or other device containing their account information. We've come a long way since the days of charging with metal coins, and the cards in your wallet may become obsolete shortly as well.

Who invented credit cards?

Credit is defined as the quality of being trustworthy. Any time people borrow something to repay, it is considered credit; that is, someone has put their faith in you to repay them. The concept of credit has existed for a long time, but it wasn't until the late 1940s that modern-day rewards credit cards were born. Since the days of trading cowrie shells, furs, and wampum, we've come a long way. It's difficult to imagine a system of trading goods such as spices or cattle, a world that exists not far in the future. For those who already have been in the miles and points hobby for a long time, even cash seems antiquated. The most rewarding method of making purchases does not necessitate any physical exchange. Simply swipe a travel credit card, start taking what you want, and save for your free vacation. In the nineteenth century, a couple of gadgets were created to represent credit. The Diners Club card, introduced in 1951, is widely regarded as the first widely used credit card. But, significantly predating that card, a man named John Biggins introduced the first look-alike of the modern-day credit card, a product you've never heard of in the mid-1940s.

Why was the credit card invented?

Flatbush National Bank's John Biggins was a Brooklyn banker. In 1946, he showed his invention, a bank card called "Charg-It," to his community members. Biggins wanted to increase the number of loyal customers at his bank. The "Charge-It" card was only available to those who had accounts with Flatbush National Bank. They could only use this bank card at participating shopping centers because it was an experiment. When a customer used the card to make purchases, the merchant would hand over the goods without asking for payment right away. The merchant would then take the sales slips to the bank and deposit them. The bank would repay the merchant and then bill the cardholder later. Around 1958, major financial institutions entered the fray when American Express and Visa became the first to introduce credit cards. Discover, JCB, and MasterCard came in second and third, respectively. Airlines didn't start creating frequent flyer programs and partnering with banks until the 1980s, giving us some more rewards to use credit cards decades later.

How did credit cards become popular?

The first widely used credit cards were designed for traveling salespeople. Customers quickly realized the cards' time-saving aspect, which boosted their popularity. Initially marketed as a convenience for use on the road, customers quickly learned the cards' time-saving aspect, which boosted their popularity. Before it was illegal, card issuers would send pre-activated credit cards to people who had never applied for one in the hopes of gaining their business.

How have credit cards changed over the years?

In 1960, IBM added a magnetic stripe to the back of a credit card, storing sensitive data like your name, card expiration date, and account number. Since then, there have been numerous attempts (many of which have failed) to make credit cards more entertaining, flashy, convenient, and prestigious. Here are some more successful examples:

- Mini credit cards meant for the keychain
- A personal picture could be added to the front of the card
- RFID credit cards allowing contactless payments
- Chip + PIN capabilities
- Digital card number for payments via mobile apps like Samsung Pay and Apple Pay

Card issuers are always looking for ways to improve security, and the best solution so far has been the inclusion of EMV computer chips. The introduction of metal-stamped cards, such as the following, is one advancement that makes no significant difference other than placing a spring in your step.

- Chase Sapphire Preferred® Card

- Chase Sapphire Reserve®
- IHG® Rewards Club Premier Credit Card
- Marriott Bonvoy Brilliant™ American Express® Card
- American Express® Gold Card

Credit Agencies

The nationwide consumer reporting agencies use your credit report to determine your credit score, which lenders use to assess your creditworthiness. The three major consumer reporting companies around the country include Equifax, TransUnion, and Experian. They use credit reports to produce a credit score. Fair Isaac's FICO score, varying from 300 (low) to 850 (high), is one of the most widely employed credit rating formulae. The better the score, the more likely you would be accepted for new credit or get a lower interest rate negotiated. This takes several variables, including your credit background, to determine your FICO score. Consumer credit agencies often don't reveal how scores are determined because no one understands how they are calculated. The agencies can have specific credit background details, and the ratings can vary from one agency to another. Your credit report reveals your payment background over the past seven years (on schedule, late, or missed).

Hard Inquiries vs. Soft Inquiries

Each time that a prospective creditor accesses your credit report and ratings, it is reported as a complex request on your account. So much of these may indicate potential creditors that you seek to open more than one line of credit, who can prefer not to lend you money. You might learn of soft inquiries, too. These arise as you check your credit report since you're not trying to create fresh lines of credit. Unlike hard inquiries, lenders don't consider soft inquiries when deciding whether to lend you money.

Types of Soft Inquiries occur when land owners conduct credit checks while attempting to rent properties or access their credit record for surveillance.

Good Credit is your Superpower

Credit ratings affect many aspects of your life. They may:

- Impact the lender's approval of the loan
- Have an impact on your interest rates and fees on the loan
- Be accessed and analyzed by employers before they offer you a new job
- Be utilized by landlords for facilitation in their renting decisions
- Be used for ascertaining your student loan eligibility, including most private loans
- Be utilized by insurance companies when you apply for insurance. These might include car or homeowners insurance

Good Credit vs. Bad Credit

Excellent credit implies you are making payments on time, on each of your accounts, before the debt is fully paid. Alternatively, lousy credit implies you've had a rough time avoiding the deal; you could not have paid the total minimum payments or made payments on schedule.

It is important to remember that adverse information generally lasts for at least seven years on the credit report.

Bad Credit

Bad credit results from:

- Late payments

- Bankruptcies
- Foreclosures
- Collections

The bankruptcies typically sit for 10 years on the credit sheet.

The positive thing is that there is still space to boost lousy credit. Observing positive credit practices will improve a poor score and help to sustain a high score.

Super Credit Tips

Given below are some credit tips:

- You must pay bills on time
- Your credit cards should have low balances
- Develop a habit of checking your credit report regularly to make sure there aren't any mistakes. Visit **annualcreditreport.com** for a free report from each of the three major nationwide consumer reporting agencies once every twelve months
- You must not carry out too many credit inquiries in a short period. You must safeguard your finances. You need to keep your financial records in proper order and be a way of fraud and scams

Student Loans and Credit

Whether they are missed or made on time, your student loan payments are also passed onto all three nationwide consumer reporting agencies. The credit card provider starts reporting on your loans soon after disbursement.

In School

Your payment sum shows as zero dollars when you are in school, and your credit status shows either pay as decided or current, indicating your credit is in good standing.

Grace Period

When you're in your grace time, the state of your account should appear to reflect your pays as agreed or current.

Repayment

You need to strictly monitor the following:

Making Payments

When you start repaying your student loans, the estimated payment sum is reflected on the credit report as defined by your repayment program. When payments are made on time per month, the student loan account may continue to be displayed as agreed or current.

Missed Payments

Your student loan payments are recorded every 30 days, be they are paid on time or skipped. When a late or missing payment has been registered, Great Lakes can not delete it from your credit records unless conditions are extenuating or it is established that you were in school, deferment, or grace time.

Default

Your loan will go into default if you skip too many payments. Defaulting on a loan reduces the FICO score, making it difficult for new credit lines to be accepted.

A good Credit Score and its Advantages

Credit is a component of your financial strength. It lets you buy the items you need today, including an auto loan or a credit card, depending on the later payment guarantee. Planning to build your credit will ensure that you get qualified for loans, especially when you need them.

There are significant advantages of a favorable credit report and a good credit score. Although certain people have concerns about being burnt with credit, it can be a handy resource when handled carefully. If you'd like to know more about the benefits of utilizing credit, continue reading to know more.

Convenience

When traveling or shopping, carrying credit cards is more advantageous than carrying cash. It also serves as a helpful transaction log. If there are a dispute and disagreement over a purchase, using a credit card may offer you a sort of bargaining power.

Use other people's money

You're using someone else's money rather than your own in the period when you purchase something on credit and when you pay the bill.

Meet emergencies

You can quickly meet contingency costs like car repairs or health needs.

Timely utility

You have the liberty and right to use something when you need it, and you pay for it at some other time in the future.

Save on interest and fees

The most significant advantage to better and outstanding credit is money saving. For starters, when purchasing a house, strong credit will save you tens or even hundreds of thousands of dollars on a mortgage loan with ease. Car loans, credit cards, private student loans, bank loans, and credit lines usually offer good-credited individuals lower interest rates. For the future, if you intend to purchase a house with a mortgage, a strong reputation may be a deciding factor in how much home you can manage and whether or not you should buy a home. But saving on interest is only one of a variety of ways the finances will benefit from having a good credit score.

Receive better car insurance rates

Insurers review the records to decide whether to cover you or not and at what prices. They use insurance scores which vary slightly from standard scores of lending. Many auto insurance providers factor in credit ratings when calculating monthly rates, in part to forecast future claims to customers. The higher your credit score, the stronger the chance at having a good offer. You can't be turned down entirely on credit alone, but if your credit score is so low, you're unlikely to see affordable premiums.

Manage your cash flow

When you buy a new product using a credit card, you do not need to pay for it instantly. Once you swipe your card, the bank sets up the money, and you reimburse it afterward. When you pay off the whole amount in full on the due date of the statement, which is a healthy way of clearing your dues, you do not have to incur any interest for such purchases. Just be sure you make the payments on your credit card on time. From the date you make the purchase, you have the period before the next closing date of the statement plus approximately three weeks until you start to pay up. It may imply three to seven weeks of interest-free loans and help you pay off your balance on a suitable date.

Avoid utility deposits

The company would usually review your credit during the onboarding process as you sign up for a new mobile phone contract or move into a new home to create utility facilities. If the ranking comes behind the company's requirements, a cash deposit would have to be set down to create an account. In a country where 78 percent of residents work paycheck to paycheck, it may be financially challenging, to say the least, to arrange for the start-up costs of utility deposits on top of transport costs. Creating a good credit history will help hold the cash in your bank account rather than the utility companies.

Getting a rental

Similar to utility companies, your next landlord might ask to pull your credit. Depending on the market, your credit could prevent you from renting.

Better credit card rewards

When you make a payment using cash or debit, you can receive nothing but the goods or services you pay for. However, with a cash back or travel rewards credit card, you'll get one to five percent or more back from each purchase to deposit into your bank account, decrease your balance with statement credits, or cover the cost of a future flight or hotel stay. You would not have access to any of the strongest credit card perks or credit card deals with bad credit. A small range of customized cards provides some incentives for individuals with poor or bad credit. But as the balance rises through the decent and outstanding ranges, you will have exposure to some incredible rewards for already completed transactions.

Emergency fund backup plan

The latest Federal Reserve survey upheld a long-known estimate that 40% of people couldn't manage to make savings for a $400 emergency. Seeing that the typical vehicle repair, home maintenance, or hospital expense will potentially reach several times the amount of $400, it's a good thing that they have credit as a contingency option. Ideally, you'd have an emergency fund that would pay expenses covering at least three or six months (double it if you're self-employed). Yet, among the most equipped, realizing they have exposure to more cash, if required, through credit cards, credit lines, or other financing methods is nice.

Avoid and limit financial fraud

When you use your debit card, and anyone at a gas station, restaurant, or online steals your card code, the cybercriminal can rob all the cash from your checking account. That could leave you unable to pay the rent or mortgage without food funds, and it can take months to get back your income. If there is something, you can have it back. Your credit card theft obligation is more stringently restricted than debit. When anyone makes an illegal payment on your credit card, what you need to do is notify the issuer, and they can scrub the charge from the statement. Most payment cards have $0 liabilities for unauthorized purchases and provide further fraud prevention opportunities.

Qualify for excellent credit card deals

A good credit background can help you apply for the best credit cards with reduced interest rates, rewards, and cash back. Such rewards will allow you to start using your credit card and help conserve money — and would improve your reputation if you are making payments as and when they become due.

Purchase and travel protections

Some of the best credit cards for every purchase give you automatic insurance. Instead of paying the dealer for pricey purchase coverage, you might focus on buy protection, extended service security, price adjustment protection, and other credit card benefits. Credit cards can provide rental vehicle insurance coverage while driving, travel injury or delay benefits, missing or delayed luggage insurance, and other helpful and beneficial services that will save you a lot of time or hassle if things don't go the way you planned.

You must not underestimate the power of good credit

Strong credit will save you thousands of dollars if you make effective use of it. But on the flip side, poorly handled credit will quickly transform into an expensive, hard-to-manage undertaking. For this cause, you should make sure that you read your credit report or credit score. However, the good news is that you may develop your reputation over time to access future credit accounts you like if you have bad credit right now. Take the time to improve the account and, for decades to come, and you will reap the dividends.

Securing employment

And if they will obtain your approval in advance, certain companies will ask to see your credit score as part of your work application. Red flags like previous bankruptcies or repeated late payments might render them hesitant to extend a job offer to you; they might fear you may be distracted by such financial difficulties from the job demands. Since there are so many areas of your life where good credit benefits will be observed,

it is crucial to do everything you can to improve your credit. Paying your credit card bills in full and on schedule is a perfect way to continue, so when you look for work, housing, and insurance, benefits will set you up for success. Several companies would prefer to review the credit report's updated version, with details such as the financial background, to decide whether you are trustworthy or present a threat to the company.

Have something you can't afford right now

If you are short of funds and cannot afford to pay cash for a car or other necessary purchase, the use of credit allows you to get it now.

You can get better service on something that is bought on credit

If you fail to pay for something in full and a problem arises, it may be convenient to get the service needed.

Types of Credit

There are four types of credit:

Revolving credit or Credit Cards

This is a line of credit that you will choose to utilize until you pay it back. For that, you will make purchases as long as the balance is below the credit limit and will alter with time. The most popular form of revolving credit is credit cards.

You are granted a fixed loan cap for revolving credit so that you can create payments up to this amount. You will make a minimum payment each month, but otherwise, any part of the remaining charges will be the sum you pay up to the maximum sum. When you make a partial payment, the rest of the balance will be carried forward, or the loan will be revolved.

Charge cards

Charge cards are used almost the same way as credit cards, except they do not require you to carry a balance: every month, you have to cover your costs in full. Charge Cards have the following features:

- You have to make the whole payment every month for the charge cards
- There are no stringent limits

- Charge cards charge very high annual fees
- This charge no interest since you are required to pay in full
- Charge cards are not very popular
- Good credit is the pre-requisite for charge cards

Service credit

Your agreements with utility suppliers such as gas and electric utilities, television and broadband carriers; wireless telecommunications networks; and gyms are all credit agreements: every month, such firms offer their services to you with the expectation that after the event, you can pay for them. Modern credit rating systems, like the new FICO ® Score and VantageScore models, will incorporate your service payment background into your credit ratings, although such payments are not necessarily disclosed to the credit bureaus. The Experian Boost certainly gives you the right to exchange payment details of services and mobile phones so that they can be taken into consideration in credit scores relying on Experian data.

Installment credit

Installment loans are a fixed quantity of money you have been loaned to use for a specific reason. Installment credit is a loan for a fixed amount of money that you plan to repay over a sequence of equivalent monthly payments (installments) over a specified period, plus interest and fees. Revolving lending includes student loans, auto loans, and mortgages.

Credit Card vs. Charge Card

A charge card functions as a form of credit card, allowing you to pay your balance in full at the end of each billing period instead of having regular minimum balance payments for many months. Charge cards require you to be accountable for your expenses because you have to pay off your balance every month. On the other side, a credit card allows you to provide a revolving balance that you can repay over some time. The affordability of small minimum payments draws customers, and some easily slip into credit card debt.

Some charge cards have no fixed credit limit, which allows you an almost unlimited amount of purchasing capacity. On the other side, credit cards have a fixed balance cap calculated when you're accepted for the credit card. The maximum limit always remains the same until you are accepted for a raise in the credit limit, or the credit card issuer decreases the credit limit. Penalties can apply if you surpass your credit cap to obtain a charge card; you usually need to have outstanding credit. You might get entitled to credit cards, though, even with a lower credit score.

Important Credit Card terms

Not all credit cards are the same. Your job is to analyze the pros and cons of credit cards when choosing the right one for you.

Interest Rates

The cost of borrowing capital interests. In general, lenders charge a certain amount to the account's average regular balance, which is considered the interest rate. The interest rate is charged every month to the unpaid balance. Credit cards will have varying interest levels on multiple forms of transactions, such as purchases or cash advances; just make sure that you understand the fine print.

Fees

Most credit cards charge fees; however, not all cards charge the same fees. You need to fully understand what fees you are responsible for.

The most common fees are:

Annual Fees

These fees are similar to a membership fee. Typically, the issuers charge you once a year for having a card.

Transaction Fees

Transaction fees are activated when a cash advance facility is utilized.

Balance Transfer Fees

When you transfer balances from one credit card to another, you are charged balance transfer fees.

Late Payment Fees

These fees become applicable when a payment is made after the due date.

Over-Credit-Limit Fees

When your spending goes beyond your account's credit limit, these fees are levied on your account.

Return Item Fees

Fees on return items may be paid if the payment for inadequate funds is retrieved.

Here are some basic facts and terms about the credit one needs to be aware of:

Credit Limit

The maximum balance you can have on your credit card is your credit cap. Your lender establishes this, depending on your financial background and earnings.

Balance

Like a credit card, a balance is how much you owe on a revolving credit account. Consider keeping this as small as possible to stop going too close to the credit limit.

Credit Score

It is the total amount you may take as a loan on revolving credit card accounts.

Annual Percentage Report

It is the cumulative interest and other charges payable on any outstanding part of the balance. These are calculated on a yearly average and represented as a percentage. You will be better off with a lower number.

Credit Report

The credit report is an extensive and comprehensive account of the credit use records. Lenders and other firms view it to assess how good you are with resources.

Minimum Monthly Payment

It is the minimum dollar amount that needs to be paid every month to ensure your revolving credit account's good standing.

CHAPTER 5: Secrets The Card Issuers Don't Want The Customers To Know

When comparing the credit cards, you'll probably look at the fees, rewards, and APRs, as well as the cardholder agreements if you are smart. Even so, none of this will tell you the whole story. However, there are many things that credit card companies wouldn't tell you about that may affect your cardholder experience. Credit cards can also be challenging to understand. If you use them correctly, they can be powerful tools, but they can become dangerous weapons if you're not careful. Furthermore, every card contains a slew of fine print that you probably aren't aware of and that your banks would prefer you didn't know about. Here are a few things your bank won't tell you about your credit card.

Your interest rate can change at any time

Although card issuer might advertise an annual percentage rate (APR) or a range of APRs for a given card, the interest rates are not final. They can change for a variety of reasons. Few cards offer new cardholders an introductory zero % APR for 12-

15 months, after which card's APR would generally switch to more standard APRs. Cardholders who end up making a late payment may also be charged higher penalty APRs. It's also possible that the card issuer will re-evaluate the rates and decides on raising them. The prime rate, which banks measure to ascertain the lowest interest rates that can be offered to borrowers with excellent credit, is tied to the majority of credit card interest rates. The credit card's interest rate may change if the prime rate rises or falls, & the card issuer is not supposed to disclose to you if it uncovers the possibility in the cardholder agreement. The card company is also under no obligation to notify you if the APR rises due to late payments or the end of the promotional period, assuming this is spelled out in the cardholder agreement you agreed to while signing up for the card. You may also receive a forty-five days notice of inevitable increase in some cases. You are not obligated to accept; however, the card issuer would close your account if you refused.

A late payment on one card could affect your APR on other cards

Even before Credit Cards Act 2009, the credit card issuers would charge you a penalty APR if you have just one late credit card payment, even if it was on a different card. This practice has been curtailed by 2009 law, but it has not been eliminated. While 1 card issuer can't charge you penalty APR just because you paid late to some other credit card issuers, if you make a single late payment to that issuer, you will be penalized across all cards with the issuer. If you've 3 credit cards with the same issuer and make late payments on any 1 of them, the issuer may apply penalty APR to all 3 cards, even if you have only ever made one late payment. Making all of the payments on time and avoiding charging a thing to the cards you know that you won't pay back the full amount at the end of the month is a simple way to avoid this. However, if you already have credit card debt, it's something to keep in mind.

Balance transfers and cash advances are more expensive than you think

You would have heard of the balance transfer card that offers a 0% APR for a limited time to help people with credit card debt pay off their debt. This is a great way to bring the debt under control, but it isn't free. You'll usually have to pay balance transfer fees, which may be upto 5 % of the transferred balance, leaving you with more considerable debt to repay. Before you proceed, remember to read the cardholder agreement & fully comprehend how much balance transfer would cost you. Fees for cash advances can be in the form of dollar amount and percentage of the amount you're requesting.

Furthermore, unlike purchases, cash advances could be subject to higher APR, & they begin to accrue interest immediately. This may lead to a downward spiral of credit card debt. It will help if you think twice before proceeding.

You have more power than you think

The Credit card issuer competes fiercely for customers and staying financially viable means keeping them happy. So, If you've good or even excellent credit —score of 700 or higher is considered good or excellent, and you do not like something regarding a credit card, then you can easily switch. A card issuer is willing to work on things with you such as late and annual fees, credit limit, APR, payments due date, & even rewards to avoid this. Your negotiating powers are determined by credit score, & card issuers may be less willing to work with those who have bad credit or a history of late payments. However, if you have been a responsible borrower with a great credit score, it is worth calling credit card companies to see the kind of deal you will get. Make a list of what you may want.

Moreover, there is no need to be afraid of using similar cards to show what you believe you deserve. If you have been using a credit card for a long, then you need to emphasize your sincerity to the issuer. When you still fail to achieve what you need, consider following through on the threat of switching credit cards. Please read the cardholder agreement before signing up for the latest credit card and contact the cardholder if you've questions about the terms or want to discuss anything. This pays for doing your homework because any misunderstandings can cost you money in the long run.

Annual fees are negotiable

Don't want to pay the annual fee on your credit card? It's not a good idea. If you call your provider and ask nicely, they may be willing to waive the fee. They'll often say or act as if they can't do anything about it. The majority of people give up at this point. You, on the other hand, should stick around and be resilient. Customer service would always state that they are unsure if the fee can be waived. You must exercise patience and perseverance. Tell them to double-check with their boss. When the manager joins the conversation, repeat the same request. They won't want to do favors for jerks, so be confident but polite. When you are doubtful, be patient, polite, and persistent until you receive a direct response from the card's manager. They frequently prefer to keep loyal customers, so waiving the annual fee to keep one is a no-brainer. That being said, it doesn't always work, so your results may vary, but it's worth a shot.

There is no need to cancel the card

You don't have to cancel the card if you don't want to pay the annual fee, but you don't want to cancel the card because you want to keep your credit clean. Ideally, you've already had the above discussion. You can ask for a different version of the card that does not require an annual fee.

There is no need to spend money

You don't have to spend a lot of money to hit credit card sign-up bonuses and earn many miles or points if you want to reach the minimums on your card. The infamous trick of buying $1,000 worth of coins from the US mint no longer works, but there are other options. You can use other methods to effectively spend money on credit cards and earn points and miles without having to pay a lot of money upfront.

The Vanilla Card Churn Strategy

You buy $500 reload cards and load them up. There is a $3.95 registration fee for each. Typically, you can load up to $5,000 on multiple cards. In other words, you paid $39.50 for 5,000 miles. That works out to a mileage value of .008 per mile, which is excellent considering most miles are worth around .002. The money from the vanilla cards is transferred to a bluebird debit card, which is then used to pay off the credit card debt.

The Paypal Load Strategy

This is equivalent to the vanilla, except that you can use it in the Paypal account instead of paying the obscenely high credit card and international fees that Paypal charges. If you have international employees, loading up a Paypal reload card and paying them with that balance is often less expensive than paying an international plus credit card fee if you attempted to use your credit card directly on the site. There are always more of these on their way.

By using your credit card, you can travel for free

You can start doing some pretty intelligent things if you start accumulating sufficient miles in the various mileage bank accounts. Sure, you can redeem those points for cash, but converting them to miles allows you to book a round-the-world ticket for a few hundred dollars instead of thousands.

You can use the same card twice

You can always sign up for a card twice if it offers you good benefits. You can reapply and have the annual fee waived if you wait 9-18 months. This is ideal for mileage-accumulating credit cards with large signup bonuses. You could get twenty-five thousand to fifty thousand bonus points from each card, and that too without paying the yearly fee if you cycle the cards every nine to eighteen months.

You can get a signup bonus and close the account

Credit card companies frequently offer large signup bonuses to attract customers to sign up for a new credit card. Those bonuses alone can be worth tens of thousands of dollars.

You can get a lower interest rate if you ask

You will incur fees and potentially an excessive interest rate if you make a late or missed payment. Those fees can add up quickly, and higher interest rates could even quickly lead to higher debt. Some banks are willing to lower the interest rate or waive a fee in exchange for your business. All you have to do is call them and politely inquire.

Issuers make a ton of money from interchange

A complicated series of electronic communications and charges happens every time you use a debit or credit card. The merchant must pay a fee of around 2% to 5% of the entire transaction. The card issuer, banks, as well as payment processing networks all share this fee. Your credit card issuer makes billions of dollars in profit each year thanks to those processing fees. You can open a credit card with no annual fee and never pay interest, but if you use it frequently, your bank will make a lot of money. Keep this in mind because it is an impetus for banks to want to keep you on board, even if it implies waiving an annual fee or occasionally throwing in a bonus.

You can convert a card to one with no annual fee

If you don't want to keep paying an annual fee on a credit card, closing the account can harm your credit score. You can call the issuer and request that the card is converted to a no-fee card, and they will usually comply.

A Perfect Credit Score is a Gateway to Free Travel

The perfect travel rewards credit cards are only available to those with excellent credit. If you meet the requirements, you can earn bonuses ranging from fifty thousand to one hundred thousand miles for opening a new card and spending few more thousand dollars on it within the first few months. Some loyalty programs include hotel and airline transfer partners who are willing to work with you. Some companies give money back on travel purchases. Others still let you book travel using your points directly through the issuer's travel portal, with no blackout dates or limitations.

They're desperate for your business

Banks are in financial trouble, despite making substantial annual profits. For starters, marketing to consumers and attracting new clients is expensive for banks. Advertisements on television and in print are costly. Direct mail is also an option. Only a tiny percentage of people read junk mail or respond to offers for new credit cards or balance transfer deals.

Furthermore, banks are expected to lose tens of billions of dollars in annual fees as a result of a slew of regulatory changes over the last year or so, as well as new laws such as the CARD Act (officially known as the Credit Card Accountability, Responsibility, and Disclosure Act), that also governs credit card issuers. All of this has made banks even more desperate to find new revenue streams, which puts people with excellent credit ratings in the driver's seat. If you have good credit, banks will go to great lengths to win your business, especially when it comes to credit cards that offer travel rewards, cashback, and other perks. In 2010, the credit card industry experienced a roller-coaster ride. Because there is so many tempting credit card offers to choose from, you can pick and choose the best ones. It will also allow you to enter into negotiations with credit card companies in ways you have never been able to before.

They are willing to forgive you at least once

When it comes to negotiating, have you ever been pricked by one of those troublesome $35 late fees because your payment didn't arrive on time at your credit card company? Most people are unaware that this fee can easily be waived by calling the credit card company and requesting that the charge be removed from the monthly statement. You must have a good track record of paying the bills on time to make a successful request. If you call your credit card company after missing four of the last dozen payments that were due, you're not likely to get a sympathetic ear on the other end of the line. In contrast, if you have a good payment history, most banks give their customer service representatives the authority to waive a late fee once a year. Let's say you were on vacation and forgot to mail your payment, or you were simply too preoccupied with work, or you assumed the spouse had sent in the credit card bill. In any case, if the failure to pay was a one-time blunder, the credit card company will most likely forgive you. However, it will only work if you submit a formal request.

Simply call your creditor and explain your situation briefly to get the late fee waived.

You can negotiate a lot more

When you are negotiating with the credit card company, you can accomplish more than just getting a late fee waived. When most people think about credit card negotiations, they imagine themselves requesting a lower interest rate. While that is an excellent place to start, there is a slew of other questions you can ask your credit card company. Among them are the following:

- Change the payment due date (so that all of your bills aren't due at the same time)
- Change your account status from "past due" to "current" • Remove a negative mark from the credit report
- Accept partial payments in place of the total amount due Forego the annual fee on a credit card

If you are a good-paying customer, each of these requests will be given a lot more weight. Even if your credit score isn't perfect, there's no harm in trying for what you need.

They can only raise the rate for six months

Don't be discouraged if you've been hit with a higher interest rate because you were late on a previous credit card bill. That default or penalty interest rate only has to last six months. One of the Card Act provisions is that banks are limited in how long they can charge you "default rates" after you've missed a payment. Default rates are only allowed to be charged for six months if you pay the credit card bill on time during that time.

Your credit card company must restore the interest rate to its original level after six months.

Interest backdating

Some credit card companies charge interest beginning on the purchase date rather than when the transaction is posted into your account. Finding a new card issuer or always paying the bill in full by the due date are two options.

Two-cycle billing

When you shift from paying in total to carrying a balance from month to month, do you run into this problem? You have the option of switching issuers or paying the balance in full at any time.

The right to setoff

When you opened the deposit account, you may have agreed to allow the bank to take the funds if you default on your credit card. The solution is to keep your accounts separate and avoid delinquencies.

Interest rate hikes are retroactive

When the low "teaser" interest rate period ends, your existing balance may be subject to a higher rate. The only options are to pay off the account in full well before the rate rises or to close it.

Shortened due dates

Most credit card companies give you a 25-day grace period to pay off new purchases without incurring finance charges. For customers paying in full monthly, some lenders have reduced the grace period to 20 days. You should request that they return to 25 days.

Eliminating grace periods

That offer you got in the mail might not be so fantastic after all. The most common "string" is that there is no grace period on the card. Even if you pay on time, you will be charged fees for everything you buy. You simply must decline the request that appears to be too good to be true.

Disappearing benefits

Many lenders entice you to sign up by offering you additional benefits. Without the fanfare that accompanied their introduction, some lenders cut back on these extras. You should read all notices concerning account changes and, if necessary, switch cards.

Fewer rights on debit cards

Problem purchases made with a debit card cannot be "charged back," as you can with a credit card. If lost or stolen debit cards are not reported within 60 days, they may be subject to unlimited liability for losses. This differs from the $50 credit card maximum liability. You should be familiar with your card. Is it a debit or a credit card? They can be mistaken for one another.

Double fees on cash advances

A transaction fee of up to 2.5 percent of the amount borrowed on a cash advance is possible. Be wary of cards that claim to have "no finance charges." Transaction fees may still apply. Cash advances must be kept to a minimum.

Misleading monthly minimums

The longer you make payments, the more money the lender makes from finance charges. You must make it a habit to pay as much as you can each month.

Interest from day one

When you don't pay in full each month, you don't get the twenty to twenty-five-day grace period with no finance charges. When calculating interest, look for cards that do not include new purchases.

CHAPTER 6: Materialize Your Life Dreams By Building Excellent Credit Scores

Cash plays a significant part in achieving the aspirations of life. Creating good credit will help you open the door to get a vehicle, start your own company and purchase your own house. Apartment managers also review credit scores to ensure a transparent background of paying on time with a prospective renter. If you don't have a credit background, they will give the apartment to anyone with a good history. You can have credit accessible as you create the credit background to help you get the stuff you need for emergencies and unexpected expenditures. When consumers and firms can borrow capital, productive economic transactions and the economy can expand. Credit allows companies access to the products they need to manufacture the goods they purchase. A company that couldn't borrow cannot purchase the equipment and raw materials or pay the workers it wanted to produce goods and prosper. Credit also allows customers the opportunity to purchase items they like. Many things are too costly for most people to budget for all at once, from vehicles to apartments. With cash, you can pay over time while receiving vital goods and services as you need them. Although credit has a significant role to play in maintaining a functioning economy running, you can often question why you need credit as a person. Loans are a critical aspect of life for many. Loans may help create capital by encouraging people to do stuff like paying for education, increasing earning power, purchasing a house, gaining from growing property prices, or beginning a company. During an emergency, getting access to credit may be helpful.

When unexpected costs happen, or you require anything that you can not manage, it may be a lifesaver to borrow. Accessing loans is relevant in today's culture for another reason:

consumer credit reporting. Creditors also disclose credit reporting agencies' conduct, including Equifax, Experian, and TransUnion, when you borrow capital. Data regarding your financial conduct, such as whether you make loan payments late or not, is aggregated to produce credit reports and analyzed to build credit scores. Lenders use specific assessments and ratings when deciding how dangerous it can be to lend to you. It would help if you had credit to build the credit background. And why exactly do your credit reports and credit scores matter? A credit score has a substantial impact on almost all financial purchases. Your credit scores have an impact on your ability to receive additional loans. You would be less able to apply for loans or insurance if you mismanage your account and receive a bad credit score. Furthermore, you are likely to wind up with a high-interest rate loan with bad terms and conditions.

How Credit Works

Credit means to borrow capital today to purchase something, understanding you'll have to pay that back eventually, usually with interest. This can help you maintain financial flexibility and build your credit when used correctly. You will pay at least the amount on your credit card statement per month, but you can pay an extra amount also. If you don't pay back all the money per month, interest would be charged to you, which is a percentage of the outstanding debt. How you pay your bills and control your finances impacts your financial background, influencing your potential opportunity to access certain forms of credit. With credit, all is tracked and measured. And note, debit and prepaid cards don't help with credit creation. Creditors may have gauged the creditworthiness by credibility alone during the last centuries. This approach was naturally arbitrary and vulnerable to distortion, exploitation, and prejudice. Creditors these days prefer an extra objective approach. So In U.S., they usually look at the financial history — the background of borrowing & repaying the funds — as the first phase in deciding how to give credit to you. The credit history summarised in files called credit reports are compiled by 3 independent credits bureaus —TransUnion, Experian, and Equifax. The credit unions, banks, credit card issuers & other creditors submit the loan and interest records to credit bureaus voluntarily. The following information is included in the credit report:

- Your total number of the credit cards accounts, their respective credit limits & current excellent balances
- Your accumulative loans & how much you've paid back
- A monthly chronological record of your payments history: whether they were missed, paid late, or cleared timely
- More considerable financial losses, such as foreclosures on homes, auto repossessions & bankruptcies

Creditors also use a 3-digit number known as credit score just as the first move in determining whether to give credit or not as a measure to further narrow down their lending decisions. The credit score distills the details found in the credit reports as to something easy to understand & reasonably does that that minimizes prejudice. Sophisticated algorithms are known as the credit scoring model, measure the credit scores by performing sophisticated mathematical reviews of the credit file's contents. Numerous models, like FICO ® Scores & the Vantage Score ®, measure scores in a different way, but both assign more excellent scores to people whose financial background renders them objectively more worthy of credit than the ones with the lower scores.

Why Do You Need Good Credit?

Substantial credit is required if you're going to borrow the money for significant transactions like a vehicle or a house. Or you maybe wish to take advantage of the ease and buy-protection that a credit card may give. A more excellent credit score will indicate improved interest rates and credit card conditions. Most card issuers often hold a better value for consumers for their most tempting loyalty cards. Lenders are not the only people who worry about the account records & credit scores. The Landlords will review your background as they want to rent your apartments or assess how high-security deposits are expected. In calculating the prices, insurance firms will use the credit scores just as criteria. Utility companies will test the credit before they agree to allow you to open an account or even borrow equipment. Prospective employers can make a hiring decision using the information contained in the credit reports.

You may also use the credit report to validate your identification and specific purposes specified by federal legislation. Credit is a device that will help you shop & pay for items you need today, over time. A significant part of healthy financial health is the creation & building up of good credits over time.

Credit Scores

A credit score of 700 or greater is usually considered perfect for a score between 300 and 850. A ranking of 800 or higher on the same scale is considered outstanding. Most credit scores fall between 600 and 750. Higher scores enable more robust credit choices and will allow creditors to be more optimistic on your repayment potential loans as agreed. Creditors, from banks issuing home loans, credit card providers, and also car dealerships funding vehicle sales, utilize credit scores to make choices on whether or not to offer the credit (such as a credit card or loan) and what the conditions of the contract (such as interest rate or down payment) would be. There are various kinds of credit scores. Two of the more popular forms of credit scores are FICO ® and VantageScore scores, although there are also industry-specific scores.

A Good FICO® Score

FICO ® Scores, produced by the Fair Isaac Company, are among the most well-recognized credit score forms. Most lenders utilize FICO ® Scores and often vary between 300 **and** 850. A FICO ® score of 670 or higher is considered a good credit score, while a score of 800 or higher is deemed outstanding.

FICO® Score Ranges

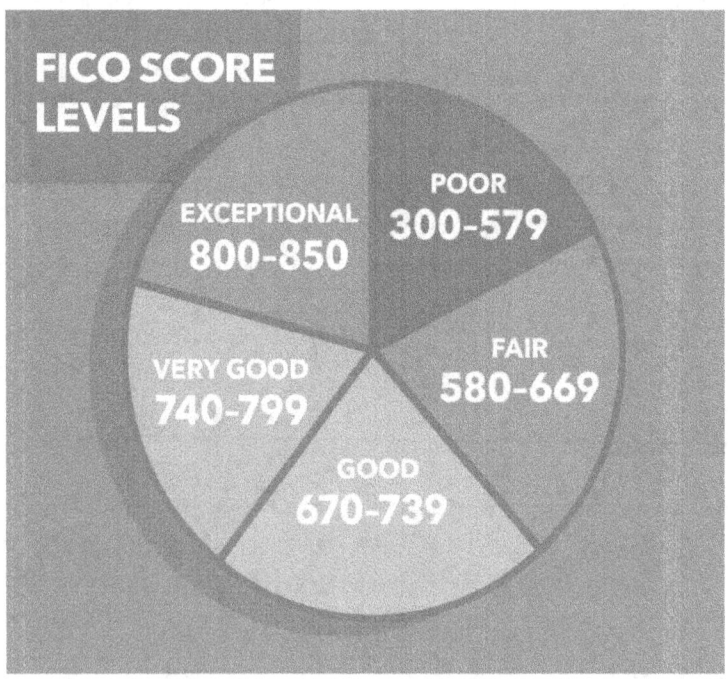

Credit Score	Rating	% of People	Impact
300-579	Very Poor	16%	Credit applicants may be expected to pay a fee or deposit, and applicants with this credit rating will not be accepted.
580-669	Fair	17%	Applicants with these scores are construed as subprime borrowers.
670-739	Good	21%	Just 8 percent of applicants are expected to become severely delinquent in the future in this score category.
740-799	Very Good	25%	Applicants with these scores have more likelihood of receiving better than average rates from lenders.
800-850	Exceptional	21%	Applicants with scores in this category are at the top of the list for the lenders' best rates.

A Good VantageScore

VantageScores are yet another type of credit score that lenders generally use. Three main credit bureaus developed the Vantage Score: Experian, TransUnion, and Equifax. The latest Vantage Score model 3.0 makes use of ranges between 850 and 300. A VantageScore of 660 and above is considered significant. On the contrary, a score above 780 is regarded as excellent.

VantageScore 3.0 Ranges

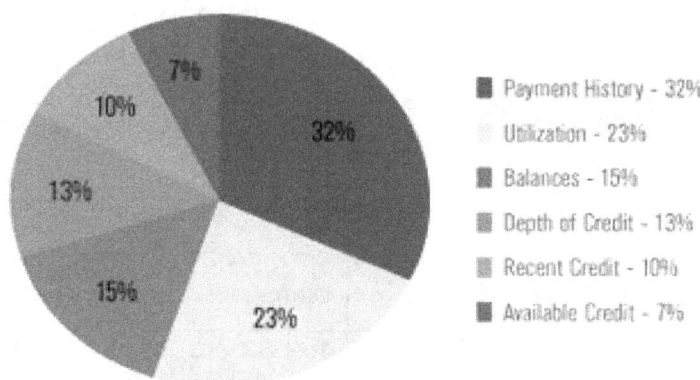

CONSUMER CHARACTERISTICS CONTRIBUTING TO A VANTAGESCORE

- Payment History - 32%
- Utilization - 23%
- Balances - 15%
- Depth of Credit - 13%
- Recent Credit - 10%
- Available Credit - 7%

Credit Score	Rating	% of People	Impact
300-499	Very Poor	5%	Credit Applications for this score will not be approved.
500-600	Poor	21%	Applicants may be eligible for specific credit, but rates may be undesirable and subject to requirements such as higher sums of down payment.
601-660	Fair	13%	Applicants may be approved for credit but with less competitive rates.
661-780	Good	38%	Applicants who are likely to be accepted at competitive rates for credit.
781-850	Excellent	23%	Applicants with an enhanced probability of receiving the best rates along with the most favorable terms on credit accounts.

VantageScore 3.0 vs. other scoring models

Credit factor	VantageScore 3.0	VantageScore 4.0	FICO® Score 8	FICO® Score 9
Utilization rate	Very important	Very important	Very important	Very important
Historical utilization rate and payment info (trended data)	Zero impact	May affect your score	Zero impact	Zero impact
Collection accounts	Ignores paid collection accounts	Paid collection accounts are ignored. Medical collection accounts that are less than six months old are ignored. Weighs outstanding medical payment records lower than other collection forms accounts	Small-dollar "nuisance" accounts that had an original balance of less than $100 are ignored. Treats medical collection accounts as all collection accounts, like those with a zero balance	Paid collection accounts are ignored. Weighs outstanding medical reports below other forms of collection accounts

Learn to correctly use Credit Scores offered by three Credit Bureaus

Lately, the world of credit ratings has been rocked by big stories. The Consumer Financial Protection Bureau forced TransUnion and Equifax to pay more than $23 million in penalties and compensation for misleading customers regarding the value and actual expense of credit scores they sold to buyers. The orders clarified that the credit score models, which borrowers most commonly use, are produced by Fair Isaac Corporation (FICO). The scores provided by TransUnion and Equifax, by comparison, utilized proprietary rating models, often referred to as "educational credit scores." The term comes from the notion that such scores typically help inform customers about their credit scores. The issue, the CFPB argues, was that TransUnion and Equifax deceived customers by claiming that the educational credit scores they provided were the identical scores that borrowers used to make lending decisions. And, according to the CFPB, borrowers never used such scores to make credit recommendations. Therefore, it is appropriate to study the credit scores, how they function, and which most relevant scores.

Multiple Credit Scores

While some may be surprised, every user has several credit scores. There are numerous explanations for using multiples scores. First, at each of the three main credit agencies- TransUnion, Equifax, and Experian, most customers have credit records. Although credit information from one credit bureau to the next will usually be the same, there are always slight variations. Such variations will result in three distinct credit scores, even if the same credit scoring model produces the score. Second, there are several common types of credit scoring. There are FICO ratings and educational credit scores according to directives given by CFPB. There are also more differences within each of these. Orders released by the CFPB note that since 2011, FICO has introduced more than 60 separate scoring models. They have different business templates, as well as regular updates to existing FICO score models.

Credit Scores and Lenders

With the multitude of scoring models, how can we assess which score would be used by a particular lender? According to Fair Isaac, FICO scores are utilized by 90 percent of "most" US lenders. Although this helps narrow down the game, note that since 2011 Equal Isaac has launched over 60 FICO scores. You have more than one FICO Score depending on the form of loan you are applying for, and the lenders will analyze the credit risk using various variations of the FICO Score. For starters, auto lenders also utilize FICO ® Auto Scores, an industry-specific variant of the FICO Score customized to their needs. For comparison, the bulk of credit card issuers use FICO ® Bankcard Scores or FICO ® Score 8.

The FICO Score 8 is the most commonly used FICO score, however. That's correct, even though they have also released FICO Number 9.

Financing a new car

FICO® Auto Scores, the industry-specific scores are used in the number of auto financing-related credit evaluations.

Getting a new credit card

FICO® Bankcard Scores or FICO® Score 8 are the score versions used by most credit card issuers.

Getting a mortgage

Base FICO® Score versions used before FICO® Score 8 are the scores primarily used in several credit evaluations related to mortgage. About mortgage, given below are the three credit scores that lenders mostly use:

- Equifax Beacons 5.0
- Trans Union F I C O Risk Scores, Classic 4.0
- Experian or Fair Isaacs Risk Model V 2 S M

These are fancy names for FICO Scores 5, 2 & 4, respectively.

How do you see your FICO Score?

This is where the big question comes. How can we have a peek at these scores in advance before qualifying for a credit card, car loan, or mortgage? A naive reading of the CFPB's directives might cause us to conclude that when applying for loans, we can see the scores used by lenders as long as we ignore such "educational credit scores." But, much of the time, you can't. For example, Fair Isaac would give you access to the FICO scores through its myfico.com website. This would potentially grant you admission to twenty-eight of the most commonly utilized FICO ® Score. However, there is no certainty that a lender can use either of these scores. Even if you have access to them a couple of months before applying for loans, they'll have modified by the time the lender evaluates the application. That doesn't mean the FICO scores don't have any importance. It gives you a general idea of where you are standing. It will even let you know what benefits and damages your score, which is perfect for those trying to boost their FICO score. But there is no assurance that the score you display will be the same score a lender sees.

Are Educational Scores Worthless?

And this takes us to the educational scores. The Quizzle, Credit Karma, and Credit Sesame are common free credit score sites. Each gives a score dependent on various scoring models for the educational score. Some are swift to ignore such scores because most of the countless FICO templates are not focused on them. Such educational scores, on the opposite, are similar scores based on the FICO standard. They offer you a general glimpse into where the credit stands. The services do a decent job at letting you know what benefits and what damages your score. And in the end, they are safe. The trick is to maintain your score by making prompt payments, holding your credit utilization to a minimum, and applying for new credit only when you need it. Testing your performance with any of these services, a FICO, or an educational score, has the added benefit of offering you a general picture of where you are and what you might do to boost your score.

Important facts you must know about the three main credit bureaus

The 3 major customer credit bureaus are Experian Equifax and Trans Union. They collect and maintain information about you that they use to produce your credit reports, which are used as the foundation for your credit scores. The credit bureau's company gathers & holds various forms of details about you and your financial records and background. Making your credit reports, which in effect form the foundation for your credit scores, depends on this data. Yet, they are independent companies who bid for creditors 'business and use these

organizations' credit records and scores to support them in making lending decisions. But they're not the only 3 bureaus out there. You will learn about the details the credit bureaus gather, how credit offices obtain the information they use to produce the reports and scores, and how to contact them if you believe anything is incorrect.

What data do the credit bureaus include in your credit reports?

Your credit report can be regarded as a snapshot of your history as a borrower. Each of the different credit bureaus collects a few critical pieces of information to create your credit reports.

Credit account information

It included information about your different types of accounts (credit card, student loan, auto loan, mortgage, etc.), the dates these accounts were initiated, your credit limit, account balances, and payment history.

Hard and soft inquiries

These kinds of inquiries often surface on the credit reports. Hard inquiries usually arise anytime you authorize your credit reports to be reviewed by a person, organization, or credit issuer, which may momentarily lower your credit scores. Soft investigations arise while you conduct stuff such as updating your credit records which do not harm your credit.

Bankruptcy information

This relates to information regarding your filing of bankruptcy and the specific chapter.

Collection accounts

There are accounts of overdue payments transferred to a collections department.

The credit reports may contain sensitive information such as your name, address, Social Security number, and birth date.

How are your credit reports used?

The credit report database is used for estimating the credit scores. Credit-scoring models can evaluate similar details differently from the same credit report. The two rating models, FICO and VantageScore, are looking at details to assess the scores in five significant areas: payment background, loan use, financial performance, credit mix, and recent credit.

Creditors, such as credit card issuers, will still use the credit records as they decide that they can create a line of credit for you. The credit bureau can also use your filing records to determine your credit score.

How do credit bureaus get your information?

The information gathered by the bureaus comes from a variety of sources.

Information through creditors

For instance, creditors and credit card issuers may share information about the accounts and customers to the credit bureaus.

Information collected or bought by the bureaus

The credit bureaus may have to buy the data for some types of information, and For instance, a consumer credit bureau can opt for purchasing public records information and use this information when generating your credit report. A credit bureau may buy data about government tax liens or bankruptcy records.

Information sharing between bureaus

The credit bureaus are sometimes compelled to share information. For instance: **An initial fraud alert** reported by you to any one of the bureaus is required to be forwarded to the other two by the first recipient.

Why are your credit reports and scores different from bureau to the bureau?

You can note while reviewing your credit that your credit scores can differ by the bureau. The potential differences in the details that make up every report may be one explanation for this variability. Creditors are not obliged to disclose credit office detail. While all creditors choose to report, others may submit the account information to either one or two of the main bureaus rather than all three, resulting in different records being reported from bureau to bureau. Since a credit score is extracted from the specifics in a single credit report, the credit scores vary greatly based on which bureau report is being used as an information source. You can also note that your FICO credit score is different from your VantageScore — even though utilizing the same report from the same office. This is because they are two separate scoring methods that use subtly different strategies to generate the scores while reviewing the credit reports.

Why Are Credit Scores so Pivotal?

Credit scores are decision-making tools that creditors use to help them predict your chances of repaying your loan on time. Credit scores are often also referred to as risk scores because they help lenders determine how you can not repay the loan as decided. It is necessary to have good credit, as it decides how you can qualify for a loan. So that can determine the difference between hundreds and perhaps thousands of dollars of money, based on the interest rate of the loan you apply for. A decent credit score may also imply you can find your dream apartment or even get the mobile phone coverage you need. Think of your credit scores like a report card that you would check at the end of a school year, but the performance winds up inside a scoring category instead of letter grades. Unlike college ratings, though, credit scores aren't placed in your credit history. Instead, each time a lender requests it, the score is created according to their choice's credit scoring model. Through when you set a big financial target, such as being a homeowner or buying a new vehicle, your credit is likely to be a part of the image of financing. Your credit ratings will help lenders decide whether you qualify for a loan or not and how fair the loan conditions would be. Yet credit scores are not typically the only items that lenders can look for as they want to stretch your credit or give you a loan. The credit report frequently includes information that may be considered, such as the overall sum of loans you hold, the forms of credit on the record, the period you've held credit reports, and any negative marks you might have. In addition to your credit report and credit ratings, lenders may often view your overall expenditures against your monthly income (called your debt-to-income ratio) based on the form of loan you obtain.

Secrets of Credit Scores

The information that impacts a credit score depends on the scoring model being used. Credit scores are usually affected by the following elements in the credit report:

- Payment history for loans and credit cards
- Total number of late payments

- Credit utilization rate
- Type, number, and age of credit accounts
- Total debt
- Bankruptcy data
- Information on new credits accounts
- Number of inquiries for the credit report

FICO® Score Factors

Following are critical FICOScore factors:

Most influential

Payment history on loans and credit cards are the most influential FICOScore factors.

Highly influential

Total debt and amounts owed are highly influential FICOScore factors.

Moderately influential

Length of credit history has a moderate impact on your credit ranking.

Less influential

New credit and credit mix, that is, the types of accounts you have, are least influential in determining a credit score.

VantageScore Factors

Following are critical VantageScore factors:

Most influential

Payment history is the most influential parameter in your credit ranking.

Highly influential

Age & type of credit, along with the percent of credit limit used, are highly influential VantageScore factors.

Moderately influential

Total balances and debt have a moderate impact on credit score calculation.

Less influential

Recent credit behavior & inquiries, along with available credit, have a minimum bearing on your credit score.

Information not considered by Credit Scores

The credit scores do not incorporate the following information:

- Your ethnicity, color, faith, national origin, marital status, or gender. Courtesy to the U. S. Consumer Credit data protection act, legislation forbids credit score systems from recognizing these facts, any acceptance of public assistance, or the exercising of any consumer right.
- Your age
- Your occupation, salary, title, employer, employment date, and employment history. However, lenders may consider this information in arriving at their approval decisions.
- Your residential status
- Soft inquiries are typically conducted by others, such as businesses offering exclusive credit deals or the lender regularly checking the current credit accounts. Soft inquiries often arise by reading your credit report or utilizing credit reporting software offered by Experian organizations. Such inquiries do not affect the credit score.

CHAPTER 7: Creative Ways to Make Money while Using the Credit Card

Credit card debt is nothing new to Americans. According to GOBankingRates.com's 2016 U.S. Household Debt survey, the median amount owed on a credit card is $2,000. If you're one of the people who have a high credit card balance, you're probably paying interest. As a result, while your credit card company profits from the interest and fees you must pay, you lose more and more of the hard-earned money. However, there is a clever way to pay off the credit card debt: Put your credit card to good use. Sure, swiping your card at every opportunity won't make you rich overnight. However, by strategically using your credit cards, you can start generating some cash for payments. Moreover, if you're debt-free, you could even put the extra money toward a vacation or that flat-screen television you've always wanted. Here are some unusual ways to earn money with credit cards.

Get money with cash-back credit cards

Have a card that pays you to shop if you want to make money with credit cards. A cash-back credit card is a name for this type of card. Based on the type of card you get, you can earn one percent to even 5% in cash-back rewards for certain purchases. Take, for example, the Discover it card. With this credit card, it is easy to earn 5% cashback on up to $1,500 in purchases in rotating categories like gas, restaurants, and more every quarter. So, if you spend US$1,500 on eligible purchases, you'll receive $75 back in your pocket. You also get 1% unlimited cash back on all the other purchases in addition to the 5% cashback. This card also comes with a unique benefit: Discover will match all cash back earned in your first-year dollar for dollar, which can add up quickly. You can earn more money with a cash-back credit card if you use it frequently. But proceed with caution. To avoid credit card debt and high-interest charges, pay off the credit card balance in full each month. The cash-back rewards may not be worth it if you get into too much debt.

Earn bonus rewards points

The best way to make money with credit cards is to open a new card with a handsome flight mileage bonus and redeem the points for a free or heavily discounted flight. You can choose from a variety of credit cards that offer sign-up bonuses. For example, the Chase Sapphire Preferred credit card, which GOBankingRates named one of the best travel rewards credit cards, lets you earn fifty thousand bonus points after spending $4,000 on purchases with the card within the first three months of account opening. You'll have $625 in your pocket to spend on travel. As a result, you may want to use this or similar rewards cards for as many purchases as possible. And, if possible, see if paying your rent with your credit card will earn you points. Earning Points is the best way to get value - or money - from credit card use. However, many people do not charge one of their most significant monthly expenses: rent to their credit cards.

Invest your cashback

Even if you only make a few hundred dollars a year, you can put cash-back rewards to function for you and invest the money. The cash-back rewards would then grow into a sizable nest egg over time due to the power of compounding interest. Assume you receive $300 in cashback each year. If you put $300 into a savings account that pays 7% interest annually, the balance will rise to more than $4,000 in ten years. Some rewards credit cards allow cardholders to connect their cards to qualify investment accounts as an added benefit. Take, for example, the Fidelity Rewards Visa Signatures credit card, which allows you to earn an unlimited 2% cash reward and have it automatically deposited into an eligible Fidelity account, including a 529 college plan for savings, brokerage account, a retirement account, and more. Search for credit cards with no stringent categories if you want to maximize investment earnings. The more restrictions you put in place, the fewer opportunities you'll have to cash in and invest your winnings.

Sell your rewards points

If you travel frequently, travel rewards credit cards are a godsend. But what if you aren't a frequent traveler? By booking tickets for family and friends with points in exchange for cash, you could even sell your points for money. It has the potential to be a win-win situation for both parties. Your friends get a cheaper ticket.

Moreover, you get cashback at a higher rate as compared to what your bank might give you. However, before getting too excited and starting selling your unwanted rewards for cash, you should be aware of the dangers. While some rewards programs allow members to give family and friends points or rewards, selling these benefits for cash may be against the terms & conditions of some programs. So, before you sell, read the terms and conditions of the credit card rewards carefully -

and double-check that the process isn't illegal in your state.

Do your shopping online

Some credit cards permit you to earn cash back and points when you shop online as a perk. To access these savings and take full advantage of the deals, you may need to log into the credit card account. When eligible Discover card members shop through Discover Deals, for example, they can earn extra cashback. This includes 5% cashback on purchases made through LivingSocial, Apple, Wal-Mart, and other online retailers. They can also get gift cards or discounts on their subsequent purchases, such as a $25 Sam's Club gift card. Similar shopping portals are available from other credit card companies. Read the terms and conditions of any shopping portal you use and make sure you understand how the program works.

Join acorns and link a credit card

If you'd like to invest but aren't sure where to start, the Acorns app could be an excellent place to start. This investing platform invests your spare money from everyday purchases automatically. Simply create an account and connect your debit or credit card. Acorns round up all of the purchases to the nearest dollar and invest the difference, converting your spare change into cash. The funds are invested in diversified portfolios to reduce risk, and you can connect as many credit cards as you want. The amount you can earn through the app is determined by how frequently you use a linked credit card. There is a monthly fee of $1 to use the service. You can use

Acorns for free for up to four years if you're a college student with a valid.edu email address.

Get creative with expired credit cards

You can't buy anything with an expired credit card, but you can turn it into artwork and sell it. Some DIY-ers are exploring their crafty side by making handmade jewelry out of expired credit cards, which is probably a foreign concept. The profit you can make from selling these one-of-a-kind fashion items varies. If you're interested, credit card accessories can be found on Etsy.com for as little as $5 and as much as $20

Earn credit card bonuses

Bonuses and rewards from credit cards are only one part of the puzzle. Credit cards could provide a lot more value to consumers when they are used responsibly. If you don't have one or don't use it regularly, you could be wasting money. Many reward credit cards offer sign-up bonuses if you apply for a new card and meet specific criteria. Many cash-back credit cards, for example, will reward you with a couple of hundred dollars in cashback, points, or miles if you spend $500 or $1,000 within the first few months. Some credit card companies also offer long-term credit card bonuses, which you can take full advantage of. Some may, for example, give you a rebate of points or miles each time you redeem the rewards. Alternatively, you could get an annual rewards bonus which is dependent on your spending.

Use your card every day

Rewards cards, along with credit card bonuses, provide ongoing rewards on everyday purchases. You'll earn more money the more you use your card. Some credit cards offer additional rewards for specific purchases, such as groceries, gas, or dining out. Consider your spending habits when choosing the right card for you, and choose the card which will reward you the most based on the budget. Using multiple credit cards for the maximization of your rewards may be worthwhile in some cases.

Use a balance transfer credit card to pay down debt

It could prove advantageous if you started using a balance transfer credit card to save money on interest and keep more of your money if you're trying to pay off credit card debt. For a limited time, balance transfer cards give introductory 0% APR promotions, usually between six and twenty months. You could even transfer the balance from another card and pay off the credit card debt interest-free during the promotional period when you apply. Balance transfer fees, which typically range from three to five percent of the transferred balance, are familiar with these cards. However, based on the size of the balance and the interest rate on your other card, the savings may far outweigh the cost. Also, some credit cards do not charge a balance transfer fee.

Use a 0% APR card

A 0% APR credit card could even provide you with a trio of money-making prospects if you're thinking about making a large purchase or are in a financial emergency. These cards work in a similar way to balance transfer cards, but they offer 0% interest on new purchases for a set period. Most of these cards also have sign-up bonuses and daily rewards, which can help you get even more bang for your buck.

Savings

Improving your credit score can help you save a lot of money. It has the potential to save you more than $100,000. For example, a person with poor credit would pay over $68,000 more than a person with excellent credit simply because they have different credit scores. Because the difference between a good score and a bad score can be worth over $100,000, checking your score and making a plan to improve it is one of the best and easiest ways you could do.

The organization is the first step towards getting rich

The foundation of robust infrastructure is good credit. The first step is to be aware of the financial benefits of having a good credit score. After that, maximize your credit so that it yields a profit. The credit must work for you rather than against you. Good credit could even make you wealthy by allowing you to build a long-term money-saving system. The money you save due to having good credit is the best approach to your financial success.

Leverage credit to generate wealth

One way to invest in profitable opportunities is to use credit to build wealth in investment properties. Investment property generates cash flow that can build wealth and opens up more opportunities for you. To decide the best way to get started, do some research and purchase books on investing in real estate.

Become homeowner

Being a homeowner improves your credit score, demonstrates that you are an accountable spender, provides a tax deduction, and gives you an asset that you will appreciate over time, increasing your net worth. A poor credit score could even mean a difference of 1% or more in interest. Over 30 years, a 1% interest rate difference on a $300,000 home is roughly $62,658, and that's just the difference between a four percent and five percent interest rate.

Start a business

This one goes without saying, but aside from the apparent reasons, there are numerous tax write-offs available for home-based businesses. Personal credit is required to obtain business credit. If you're a first-time entrepreneur, you won't be able to get business financing except if the personal credit score is excellent & you can borrow money against it. If you're a new business owner or planning to start one, having a good credit score is critical to getting your company off to a good start.

Venture capital

Venture capital is a method of raising funds for businesses willing to trade equity in the company in exchange for funds to grow or expand. A venture capitalist also desires more control over a business and a faster return on investment. There is an unlikelihood that an investor will invest in your company if your credit is terrible and your company isn't built on a solid foundation.

Look favorable when you are applying for a job

Although having a bad credit score may not prevent people from getting a job, someone with a higher score may be chosen over you, despite your qualifications. Almost all employers will look at your credit before hiring you in today's competitive job market. Poor credit is frequently associated with a lack of accountability, honesty, along financial management skills. You might even be turned down for a job if you have bad credit. For instance, if you'd like to work in a bank, you'll almost certainly need a good credit score and no bankruptcies on your record.

Get approval for handsome loans and healthy credit limits

When it comes to applying for loans and other lines of credit,

credit scores are crucial. The higher your credit score, the lower your loan payment will be, and the easier and faster you will be approved for a larger loan. This can then complete the cycle, assisting you in growing your business or making it possible for you to invest in real estate. Before working with a mortgage or real estate broker, try and contact a reputable credit repair company to evaluate and potentially address inaccurate blemishes on your credit reports.

Insurance

You are entitled to an automatic one-year warranty extension. This usually means that you would not have to waste money on extra warranties. According to one expert, insurers discovered a link between credit score and losses and that people with higher credit scores filed fewer claims. This could be because good credit habits, such as paying bills on time and not taking on too much debt, can be transferred to safe driving and homeownership. As a result, the higher rates for higher grades.

College

People with a college education and degrees earn significantly more money than those who have a high school diploma or less. If you have good credit, the most feasible approach for cash-strapped students is to apply for student loans on a reasonable plan.

Utility Services

Utilities such as gas, electric, cable, and phone companies may waive large deposits and offer better plans if you have good credit. Credit scores directly impact cell phone pricing and service, according to nearly 58 percent of CFA respondents.

Skip the car rental insurance

So Using the rental coverage provided by the car rental agency can increase the rental cost by a few dollars per day. However, based on credit card usage, you may not need that extra insurance. As far as you are declining the coverage given by car rental companies, most major credit cards provide car rental insurance. Your rental can be paid with a credit card. Every time a car is rented, you can save tens or hundreds of dollars.

Use the discount mall

Numerous credit card companies also have "discount malls," or a group of national retailers with whom they partner to provide cardholders with regular discounts. This takes a little forethought, but you may save money on movie tickets, dining, flowers, and other items using the credit card issuer's discount malls. On the website of your credit card company, you should be able to find a list of those stores, as well as the amount of money you could save.

Earn free travel or hotel stays

You can earn points or miles redeemed for free flights or hotel stay if you use a travel rewards credit card. Free flights can be used for annual vacations, a holiday trip, or a weekend getaway. For even more savings, sign up for a reward membership with airlines and hotels linked to the rewards card. If you do not own a travel reward card, the discount mall on your credit card may have deals with car rental companies or hotels. Before actually making the travel plans, make sure to check there first.

Shop on retail cardholder discount days

Now If you only have retail credit cards in the wallet, you might be losing the money due to great interest rates and limited usage. If you use the retail cards infrequently, however, you can benefit from the rewards programs. The cards frequently provide benefits such as special days of discount for cardholders. You have to look for the retail credit card offers cardholder special discount days by looking through your rewards program or calling your card issuer. Also, sign in for retail cards only at the stores where you already shop frequently.

Extended Warranty Benefits

Buying extended warranties on electronics could save you money on repairs and replacements. The protection plans, on the other hand, are frequently expensive. Some credit cards offer free extended warranties on electronics purchases when you use them. Before you go shopping, check the credit cards to see if they offer this benefit & what you need to do to take full advantage of it.

Take Advantage of Price Adjustments

When you go shopping, you run the risk of buying something and then discovering it has been marked downer to lower price some days later. On the other hand, price protection credit cards may reimburse you for the price difference. The credit card determines the ease with which you can obtain the benefit. Then check the policy for details on how to file a refund claim & how far you've to do so.

Pay No Foreign Transaction Fees

On purchases made in other currencies, many other credit cards charge foreign transaction fees, usually three % of the transaction amount. The fees can quickly add up if you travel internationally. However, some credit cards waive foreign transaction fees. If you visit other countries regularly, a card with this feature can save you a lot of money.

Bottom line

When you're looking for a credit card that would allow you to make money, you'll probably notice that many of them have annual fees. While annual fees can reduce a credit card's value, they aren't always a bad thing. Examine the card's rewards program and other perks to see how much value you could get from it on a year-to-year basis. You could get perks such as free checked bags and also in-flight discounts with mileage rewards cards, which can help offset the cost of an annual fee. Compare the value you get from a card with no annual fee to the value you get from a card with an annual fee. An annual fee may be very worth it based on the spending habits and also how you plan to use the card. To avoid overspending, make a budget and stick to it, and always pay your monthly bills on time and in full to prevent unnecessary interest charges. Using your credit card responsibly can help you build your credit history and score, giving you more opportunities to save and earn money in the future.

Conclusion

Credit was used for the first time in 4,000 B.C. At that time, Sumerian people started establishing the world's first cities. In the Sumerian city of Uruk, interest-bearing loans were made, and early forms of financial contracts were shared. Various methods of making loans have evolved over the centuries, but the general concept remains the same: people need to have things they can't afford all at once, and credit allows them to get them. As of the year 2020, American households owed a total of $13.29 trillion, whereas businesses operating outside the financial sector owed $14.43 trillion. We use credit in various other ways than the Sumerians did, but borrowing is still a major part of our modern economy. This raises important questions about the value of credit and how to get it when you need it. Businesses and consumers can borrow money, allowing for more efficient economic transactions and growth. Credit gives businesses access to the tools that they require to make the goods we buy. If a company can't borrow, it might not purchase the machines and raw materials it needs or pays the employees it wants to produce products and profit. Consumers can also use credit to purchase items that they require. Many things have become too expensive for most people to pay for all at once, from cars to houses. Credit allows you to pay over time while still having access to important services and products when you need them. Although credit plays an important role in keeping the economy running, you may be curious to know why you would want credit as a person. For many people, loans are an unavoidable part of life. Loans can help people build wealth by allowing them to pay for college, increase their earning power, purchase a home and profit from surging property values, and start a business. Having credit available can also come in handy in an emergency. Being able to borrow money in the case of unforeseen expenses or a need for something you can't afford could be a lifesaver. In today's society, credit is essential for another reason: consumer credit reporting. Creditors frequently report the behavior to credit-reporting agencies such as Equifax, Experian, and TransUnion when you borrow money. Data on one's financial behavior, such as whether you make late or missed loan payments, is compiled into credit reports and analyzed to develop credit scores. Lenders look at these reports and scores to determine how risky it is to lend money to you. You must have credit to establish a credit history. The credit reports, as well as scores, are critical. In almost every financial transaction, a credit score plays a significant role. The credit scores have an impact on your future ability to obtain credit. You'll be less likely to be selected for loans and credit if you mishandle your credit and have a low credit score. Alternatively, you could eventually wind up with a loan with a high-interest rate and poor terms. When choosing whether or not to rent to you, landlords may run a credit check. The credit scores and reports are generally checked when you apply for a cell phone contract. Being a responsible credit card holder demonstrates your reliability. When determining what rates you'll pay, your auto insurer may also check the credit scores. Your credit score can also have an impact on your job prospects. The employer's right to request a revised credit report from the credit bureaus depends on the state you live in. Negative marks on the credit report may cause you to be denied. Credit aids in the accumulation of wealth and participation in the economy. Credit is a tool, and like all tools, it has the potential to be abused. If not managed properly, poor credit can harm many of the significant financial applications. People and businesses will be hesitant to do business with you if you have irregular borrowing behavior and low credit scores because credit scores are being used to measure your reliability. It's possible that you won't be able to have a cell phone contract in the absence of a large deposit or that a landlord will refuse to rent to you. Borrowing money costs money in fees and interest, and you can borrow more than you can repay. If a consumer does not understand how to manage the credit they have, they may pay a lot of money in interest and fines or penalties. This could end up spiraling out of control, forcing consumers to file for bankruptcy. To avoid problems, limit your borrowing and only take out loans that you can conveniently repay. It's also crucial to distinguish between "bad" debt and "good" debt, like a mortgage or student loan, which can help you build wealth over time. Because the United States is a credit-based economy, managing your life without credit can be difficult, especially if you do not have the ability and capacity to borrow. Similarly, in the absence of positive credit history, you may not be able to make essential purchases like a home or a college education. You have to learn about good credit and bad credit, know how to build your credit history, and become aware of the importance and benefits of credit scores along with credit secrets.

www.ingramcontent.com/pod-product-compliance
Lightning Source LLC
Chambersburg PA
CBHW071420210526
45465CB00001B/472